READING ACTS

CASCADE COMPANIONS

The Christian theological tradition provides an embarrassment of riches: from scripture to modern scholarship, we are blessed with a vast and complex theological inheritance. And yet this feast of traditional riches is too frequently inaccessible to the general reader.

The Cascade Companions series addresses the challenge by publishing books that combine academic rigor with broad appeal and readability. They aim to introduce nonspecialist readers to that vital storehouse of authors, documents, themes, histories, arguments, and movements that comprise this heritage with brief yet compelling volumes.

RECENT TITLES IN THIS SERIES:

Understanding Pannenberg: Landmark Theologian of the Twentieth Century by Anthony C. Thiselton

A Companion to Philemon by Lewis Brogdon

The End Is Music: A Companion to Robert W. Jenson's Theology by Chris E. W. Green

A Primer in Ecotheology: Theology of a Fragile Earth by Celia Deane-Drummond

Mimetic Theory and Biblical Interpretation: Reclaiming the Good News of the Gospel by Michael Hardin

Inhabiting the Land: Thinking Theologically about the Israeli-Palestinian Conflict by Alain Epp Weaver

Called to Attraction: An Introduction to the Theology of Beauty by Brendan Thomas Sammon

Postmodern Theology by Carl A. Raschke

Reading 1 Corinthians by J. Brian Tucker

Deuteronomy: Law and Covenant by Jack R. Lundbom

READING ACTS

JOSHUA W. JIPP

CASCADE *Books* • Eugene, Oregon

READING ACTS

Cascade Companions

Cascade Books
An Imprint of Wipf and Stock Publishers
199 W. 8th Ave., Suite 3
Eugene, OR 97401

www.wipfandstock.com

PAPERBACK ISBN: 978-1-4982-9302-0
HARDCOVER ISBN: 978-1-4982-9304-4
EBOOK ISBN: 978-1-4982-9303-7

Cataloguing-in-Publication data:

Names: Jipp, Joshua W.
Title: Reading Acts / by Joshua W. Jipp.
Description: Eugene, OR : Cascade Books, 2018 | Cascade Compan-
    ions | Includes bibliographical references and index.
Identifiers: ISBN 978-1-4982-9302-0 (paperback) | ISBN 978-1-4982-
    9304-4 (hardcover) | ISBN 978-1-4982-9303-7 (ebook)
Subjects: LCSH: Bible. Acts—Criticism, interpretation, etc.
Classification: LCC BS2625.2 J45 2018 (print) | LCC BS2625.2 (ebook)

Manufactured in the U.S.A.

CONTENTS

Acknowledgments vii

1. Reading Acts: Narrative, History, and Canon 1

2. God as the Subject of Acts 14

3. Israel's Restoration and the Messiah's
   Resurrection 31

4. The Messiah and the People of God 52

5. Surprising Expansions in the People of God 67

6. Paul—Missionary to the Gentiles 86

7. Paul—Missionary to Israelites and Kings 106

8. Reading Acts as the People of God: A Brief
   Postscript 133

Bibliography 141

Subject Index 147

Scripture Index 149

ACKNOWLEDGMENTS

I AM GRATEFUL FOR the ways in which writing this book has allowed me to reflect upon those who have taught me so much about the book of Acts. Some of them have been my actual professors with whom I have had (and continue to have) meaningful relationships (thank you to David Pao, Luke Timothy Johnson, and Carl Holladay). And others have been my teachers through the writing of books and articles which have impacted me. I think especially of David Moessner, Daniel Marguerat, Jacob Jervell, Kavin Rowe, and Loveday Alexander, though there are many others. My indebtedness to all of them will be evident to the reader even if this short book is not filled with footnotes in every instance.

Thanks to Chuck Cruise and Matthew Robertson for their careful comments and feedback on the book. And many thanks to the wonderful Jen Guo for her help in preparing this manuscript.

I am also grateful for the way in which the writing of this book has forced me to work toward keeping my arguments more accessible than is often the case in academic writing. Though they are both more than capable of reading academic prose, I have often thought of two of my closest friends when writing this book—Ryan Petersen (GOMB) and Kory Wenell. They spend the majority of their time pastoring local churches, caring for their families, and embodying a love for learning and love for people. I am deeply grateful for their friendship.

1

READING ACTS

Narrative, History, and Canon

THE ACTS OF THE Apostles tells the story of how God transformed a small group of Jewish followers of Jesus of Nazareth into a worldwide, multiethnic, geographically diverse community of people who confessed this Jesus as the once crucified but now resurrected and enthroned king of the universe. The author gives us no explicit statement concerning the purpose or purposes of Acts such as we find in the Fourth Gospel for example (John 20:30–31), but at its most basic level the story provides, as it were, the foundational story for the identity of the church. It describes, in other words, how God brought the movement into existence, the central characters and agents upon whom the church was built (esp. Peter and Paul), the gift of the Spirit, the foundational practices and virtues of the church, and the church's apostolic foundation of Jesus the Messiah.

The book of Acts is technically anonymous. The author addresses the work to someone named Theophilus and refers to his "first volume"—the book known as the Gospel of Luke (Acts 1:1; cf. Luke 1:1–4). Therefore, most agree that there is at minimum a unity of authorship between the Gospel of Luke and the Acts of the Apostles.

But who wrote our text? Church tradition, since at least the time of Irenaeus, is in agreement that the author is Luke, the companion of Paul in his missionary travels, who is referred to as "the beloved physician" (Col 4:14; 2 Tim 4:10–11).[1] This tradition, to my knowledge, is unanimous that this Luke penned our text, and it has usually drawn attention to the notorious "we" passages in Acts, which, on their surface, seem to indicate the author of Acts was an eyewitness travelling companion of the Apostle Paul (Acts 16:10–17; 20:5–15; 21:1–18; 27:1—28:16).[2] There are reasonable arguments, however, against the traditional view of authorship: Luke's Paul makes no mention of traditional Pauline themes such as justification by faith or the Pauline collection (Rom 15; 1 Cor 16:1–4; 2 Cor 8–9); the work could reflect an early second century dating based on similarities with other early second century Christian writings; surprisingly, Acts makes no mention of Paul as a letter-writer; and, of course, the work is technically anonymous. Nevertheless, while Lukan authorship of our text is not *certain*, it remains the most likely and plausible suggestion.[3] Not much will hinge on our identification of the historical author, as what we need to know will emerge as we explore how the author writes and what he says. As a result, I will refer to our author as Luke.

This companion is no substitute for the entertainment, edification, and sense of adventure offered by simply reading Acts for oneself. My hope is that this little book will provide an easily accessible guide to help you get as much as you possibly can out of your own reading experience. While the bulk of the rest of the book will consist in setting

1. Irenaeus, *Against Heresies* 3.1.1; 3.13.3; 3.14.1–4.

2. The Muratorian Fragment, which is an early list of canonical works, includes Acts and speaks of the work as penned by Luke.

3. See here especially Padilla, *Acts of the Apostles*, 21–37.

forth some of the primary themes and motifs of Acts, we should first ask the question, "What kind of book is the Acts of the Apostles?" Let me give us a few points of orientation to Acts before we delve into the major themes and movements of the book.

(1) ACTS IS A NARRATIVE

Whenever we read a text we bring certain expectations to our reading practices depending upon the kind of text it is that we're reading. A screenplay for a feature film, a newspaper article from the *Chicago Tribune*, and a novel by Philip Roth all share common features by being texts, and yet we recognize that all of them produce within us different expectations for how to read and interpret these writings. Biblical scholars have offered many proposals for the specific genre of the Acts of the Apostles, but these proposals have not led to anything close to a consensus. Luke does not use the technical terminology of "history," "biography," or "apology" to describe his work. But he does speak of his "first volume" (Acts 1:1; i.e., the Gospel of Luke) as a "*narrative* of all the things that have been fulfilled among us" (Luke 1:1b).

While Luke is certainly not claiming to write a narrative in the full sense in which contemporary literary theorists speak, the book is certainly a story or narrative account with all of the expected literary features such as plot, characters, setting, tension, and narrative resolution. The characters of Acts—Peter, Barnabas, Paul, antagonists to the church, and others—move the plot forward. The numerous speeches by these characters provide important interpretation of the events and the unfolding of the plot. The setting often dictates the behavior of the characters' actions and the particular idiom in which they speak. Repeated patterns, themes, literary fulfillments, and summary statements draw the reader's attention to Luke's particular concerns and agendas. Let's look at just a few of these narrative/literary techniques.[4]

a. **Setting** refers to the locale where the action is situated. Luke indicates the importance of setting in the very beginning of his narrative when he tells the disciples to wait in *Jerusalem* for the coming of the Spirit, which will empower their testimony "in Jerusalem, in all Judea and Samaria, and to the ends of the earth" (1:8). Interpretation of the speeches in Acts must attend to setting; for example, Paul's speech in a *synagogue* dictates a message rooted explicitly in Israel's history (13:16–41), whereas his speech before Stoics and Epicurean philosophers leads to proclamation more attuned to ancient philosophical themes (17:16–34).

b. **Characterization** is how the narrator represents the persons in the narrative. For example, Luke's antagonists are frequently characterized as greedy (e.g., 1:18; 5:1–11; 8:18–25). The apostles are often spoken of as having "boldness of speech" (4:13) and "grace and wisdom" (6:8–15).

c. The **repetition of literary motifs** gives the reader consistent reminders of how to interpret the plot. Thus, Luke provides repetitive statements at key junctures in the narrative to tell the reader that "the word of God increased and multiplied" (6:7; 12:24; 19:20). The ability to perform "signs and wonders" demonstrates the power of the Spirit (5:12; 6:8; 8:6).

---

4. See here the introduction by Powell, *What Is Narrative Criticism?* These literary features of Acts have been examined well by Tannehill, *Narrative Unity*. See also, Rothschild, *Luke-Acts*.

d. **Literary fulfillment** takes place when an event is predicted and its fulfillment is narrated within the narrative. The most obvious case of literary fulfillment occurs when the Spirit is poured out upon the believers in Jerusalem just as the risen Jesus had said (Acts 1:8 with 2:1–13). But this also takes place when Paul says "he must see Rome as well" and, of course, the book concludes with Paul's appearance before the synagogue in Rome (19:20 with 28:16–31). Subtler, but no less an indication of literary fulfillment, is Gamaliel's advice to leave the apostles alone lest "we be found to be fighting against God" (5:39); throughout Acts those who persecute the apostles frequently find their plans brought to futility or meet a gruesome death (e.g., 5:19–20; 12:20–23; 16:25–34).

e. Luke employs **summary statements** to help the reader interpret the plot. In Acts 1–5 he pens three important summary statements that give the reader a window into the common life of the church (2:42–47; 4:32–35; 5:12–16).

f. Luke also uses **simple repetition**, especially *threefold* repetition, to remind his reader of the climactic moments in the foundation of the early church. For example, the Peter-Cornelius story—the event that shows the church how non-Jews can become part of God's family—is narrated three times (10:1–48; 11:1–18; 15:6–11). Luke also repeats three times the conversion of Saul (Acts 9, 22, 26) as well as the sad statement in response to the synagogue's unbelief in Jesus as Messiah—"we are turning to the Gentiles" (13:47; 18:6; 28:28).

Attention to these literary features will, I trust, enable the reader to appreciate the joy of reading Acts as a story.

And we will have the occasion to expand on these literary features and add more as our study continues. Some have even proposed that the book of Acts should be thought of as a novel or a historical romance based on its sense of adventure, surprise, and entertaining stories.[5] One thinks of the literarily ornate story of God supernaturally bringing Peter and Cornelius the Gentile together in order to divinely sanction non-Jews as part of God's people (10:1—11:18), or of the showdown between Peter and Simon Magus (8:4–25), or the near-death prison escapes of the apostles (5:19–20; 12:1–17; 16:25–34), or Paul's sea-voyage ending in his shipwreck on Malta (27:1—28:16). Good readings of Acts, then, will not only analyze the text for theological themes but will enjoy and appreciate how Luke tells stories as a means of proclaiming the overarching story of the foundation of the church. Our study, then, will pay close attention to the literary elements of Acts with a goal of ascertaining how Acts works as a unified story about God's founding of the church.

(2) ACTS NARRATES HISTORICAL EVENTS

Various proposals for the genre of Acts have been offered. Some, rightly impressed with its similarities to Greek and Latin novels, have suggested that Acts is a "historical romance."[6] Others have suggested that Acts should be classified as something of an "epic," along the lines of Vergil's

---

5. See Pervo, *Profit with Delight*; a forerunner to Pervo who emphasized Luke's storytelling abilities was the influential commentary of Haenchen, *Acts of the Apostles*.

6. Pervo, *Profit with Delight*.

Aeneid.[7] And still others have argued that Acts is comparable to ancient biography.[8]

But most have argued, and I think rightly so, that Acts is some version of ancient historiography.[9] There are a variety of specific proposals for *what kind of history* Acts is, but there is nothing close to a consensus here. For our purposes, we should recognize that Luke almost certainly had access to a variety of sources (written and oral), traditions, and some eyewitness testimony about the events he describes. However, unlike his Gospel where we can examine his handling of sources (e.g., the Gospel of Mark and probably "Q"), we have no direct access to any of his sources for writing Acts. Nevertheless, it is clear that Luke has shaped his sources and traditions into a clear, coherent, and entertaining historical account of the creation and expansion of the early church.

Luke draws upon a host of techniques as a means of shaping this material into a coherent account that bears clear resemblances to both biblical and Greco-Roman historiography. A few of the most impressive include:

a. The major characters give speeches that function to articulate the preaching and teaching of the Christian message *and* interpret the plot/action of the narrative (e.g., 1:15–26; 2:14–41; 17:22–31). Luke's speeches, in fact, take up close to 25 percent of the entire volume.

b. Showing causal connections between historical events. For example, the persecution of the Jerusalem believers leads to their dispersal and missionary activity in the cities of Samaria (8:1–4).

7. Bonz, *Past as Legacy*.

8. Adams, *Genre of Acts*; Talbert, *Literary Patterns*.

9. Perhaps articulated most clearly by Moessner, *Luke the Historian*, 13–38.

c. Some level of concern with chronological detail. A well-known example here is Luke's indication that Paul's appearance before the tribunal in Corinth took place when "Gallio was proconsul of Achaia" (18:12–13).

d. Luke's imitation of Septuagintal (the Greek translation of the Old Testament) phrasing and wording, along with his plethora of quotations from the OT (found especially in the first half of Acts). This "biblicizing" style can be seen in small details such as Luke's penchant for "and so it came to pass" and in larger patterns such as his patterning Peter's character after Israel's prophets (especially Moses).[10]

e. Themes that pervade ancient historiographical writing, such as the theme of providence or divine sovereignty and divine retribution.[11]

f. Luke's prefaces to his Gospel (Luke 1:1–4) and his second volume (Acts 1:1), which indicate his intention to write an orderly, coherent account of the recent events that have taken place.[12]

While these are only a sampling of some of the historiographical features of Acts, they indicate, I believe, that Luke intended his account to function as history *and* he intended it to be an account of what he thought *actually happened*. He speaks of real people, places, cities, events, religions, and philosophies.[13] His consistent concern with

10. See Green, "Internal Repetition," 283–99.

11. See here the excellent work of Shauf, *Divine in Acts*; also, Moessner, *Luke the Historian*, 143–53.

12. Most have seen Luke's prefaces as indicating his intent to write some form of historiography. This, however, has been contested by Alexander, *Preface to Luke's Gospel*.

13. See further González, *Story Luke Tells*, 1–14; Padilla, *Acts of the Apostles*, 75–122.

historical verisimilitude indicates his desire to accurately report the events he claims to describe. If Luke's historical reporting is demonstrably false, this would not sit well with his stated purpose for his Gospel, namely, to "write an orderly and careful account . . . so that you may know the certainty of the things about which you have been instructed" (Luke 1:3b–4). Luke's stated purpose, then, is that his audience would have some level of certainty and confidence in the truth of what he narrates. This by no means should cause us to uncritically underestimate Luke's creative shaping of the events and speeches he passes on. The ability to discern Luke's theological agendas, literary patterns, or uses of rhetoric neither invalidate nor confirm the historical reliability of the events Luke narrates. But where Luke's historical information can be verified or tested, his description of purported events comes out looking reliably accurate.[14] The focus of our study, however, will not be to either prove or to discount Luke's historical reliability, but rather to enter into the story world of his account of the creation and growth of the church.

(3) ACTS UNIFIES THE CHRISTIAN CANON

The book of Acts has served a variety of purposes as sacred Scripture within the church's canon. One of the most significant purposes has been the way in which Acts has functioned as a bridge between "Gospel" and "Apostle."[15] Stated differently, the book of Acts has provided a connecting link or bridge between the stories of Jesus (in the Fourfold Gospel) and the letters of the Apostle Paul, in the first instance, as well as the so-called Catholic Epistles of Peter, James, and others. Acts can function as the continuation of the ac-

14. Keener, *Acts*, 1.166–220.
15. Wall, "Acts of the Apostles," 16–24.

counts of Jesus in the Fourfold Gospel. The book of Acts clearly served the church father Irenaeus well, for example, in his opposition to Marcion. Acts portrays Paul and the Jerusalem apostles as unified in theology and mission, depicts Paul and the earliest church as deeply rooted in God's covenant dealings with Israel, speaks of Paul repeatedly as Torah observant (chs. 21–26), and contains a speech of Paul warning against false teachers making their way into the church (Acts 20:18–35)—an event that for Irenaeus was being fulfilled in Marcion's heretical teaching.

For many contemporary Christian readers, the book of Acts has continued to function as the canonical glue that holds together the Old Testament and the New Testament, Jesus and his apostles, Paul and Peter, and the Gospels with the Apostolic Letters.[16] It is through the book of Acts that the reader has access to narrative accounts of Paul's travels and missionary endeavors in locations to which Paul's canonical letters are addressed (e.g., Thessalonica, Corinth, Philippi, Ephesus). Thus, for the canonical reader there is a continuity of identity between the Paul of Acts and the Paul of the Epistles. Many of the earliest Greek codices actually preserve an order that places Acts before the Catholic Epistles with Paul's Epistles coming next. Thus, the canonical placement of Acts in these codices would seem to follow the order of Acts (first the Jerusalem apostles in Acts 1–12 and then the Apostle Paul in Acts 13–28).[17]

For our purposes, however, I think it is worth exploring in more detail the relationship between Acts and the Gospel of Luke. It is true that there are no ancient manuscripts where the Gospel of Luke and Acts appear placed together "ready for reading as a continuous whole."[18] Some

16. See especially Smith, *Canonical Function of Acts*.

17. Goswell, "Order of the Books," 233–35.

18. Using the language here of Parsons, *Acts*, 13.

have used this argument, then, to suggest that we cannot verify that Luke and Acts were published together or that Luke intended for the two texts to be read with one another.[19] And those responsible for our Christian canon must have felt it perfectly justifiable to maintain an order that did not place Luke and Acts with one another. Those who have argued against the literary unity of Luke-Acts have raised important questions and have rightly called attention to the multiplicity of ways in which Acts can justifiably be read. However, without denying other legitimate readings, I suggest that the book of Acts is illuminated most powerfully when it is read as Luke's second volume or sequel to his Gospel.

There are a variety of ways in which Acts is presented as continuing the story of Jesus from the Gospel of Luke. For example, the apostles are characterized according to the pattern of Jesus in that they share the same Spirit, perform signs and wonders, proclaim the gospel with authority, and are rejected by the people. Acts often narrates the fulfillment of something that was predicted in the Gospel. For example, John the Baptist prophesies that a coming one will baptize "with the Holy Spirit and fire" (Luke 3:16), and this is fulfilled in Acts when the Spirit is poured out upon the disciples with flames of fire (Acts 2:1–4). Simeon proclaims that the coming of Jesus will be of saving significance for both Israel *and* the nations (Luke 2:30–32), but this promise is not made good until Peter's encounter with Cornelius in Acts 10, which initiates the mission to the Gentiles.

When we turn to the introduction of Acts in 1:1–11 we see good reasons for the view that Acts is continuing the story of Jesus in the Gospel of Luke. As we have seen, the opening words of Acts 1:1–2 make direct reference to

19. Parsons and Pervo, *Rethinking the Unity*; Rowe, "History, Hermeneutics."

Luke's "first account" written to Theophilus and serve to create some level of continuity between Acts and his Gospel. Luke immediately draws the reader's attention to some form of continuity between the Gospel and Acts through his concise but effective use of the rhetorical technique of recapitulation.[20] In brief summarizing form, Luke reminds the reader of *some* of the most important aspects of Jesus's ministry and teaching. The reader of Acts, for example, is already familiar, by way of the Gospel, with Jesus's heavenly ascension (Luke 24:50–53; Acts 1:2, 9–11), Jesus's election of the apostles (Luke 6:12–16; Acts 1:2), Jesus's dining practices (Luke 24:28–35; Acts 1:4), the kingdom of God as the content of Jesus's proclamation (Acts 1:3, 6), the death and resurrection of Jesus (Luke 23–24; Acts 1:3), John's ministry of water baptism and anticipation of a greater one to come (Luke 3:16; Acts 1:5), and the promise of the outpouring of the powerful Holy Spirit in Jerusalem (Luke 3:16; 24:49; Acts 1:4–5b, 8). The frequency of the allusions to Luke 24:36–53 direct the reader to the ending of Luke's Gospel and thereby indicate that with Acts 1:1–11 *Luke is transitioning to a development of a new stage within the same story begun by the Gospel.*[21] And this is even hinted at with the precise language of Acts 1:1, which speaks of Luke's first account as narrating everything that "Jesus *began to do and to teach.*" The implication, then, is that Acts will go on to describe how Jesus *continues* to act, teach, and accomplish his purposes in this new stage of his ministry.

20. Johnson, *Acts of the Apostles*, 28.

21. Tannehill, *Narrative Unity*, 11.

REFLECTIONS

1. Does Acts strike you as having the typical features of a narrative or story? Have you read Acts before with attention to its literary, narrative dynamics?

2. What would be missing from the Christian canon if Acts was absent? How would this influence our reading of Paul's Epistles? Or our reading of the Synoptic Gospels?

2

GOD AS THE SUBJECT OF ACTS

ACTS IS ABOUT GOD. As Luke's prologue to his Gospel makes clear with its claim to recount "the things that have been fulfilled among us" (Luke 1:1), Luke-Acts is from beginning to end a narrative construal of God and God's activity.[1] Characters respond to and reject divine activity, Israel's Scriptures are evoked to give witness to God's acts, the Spirit enables characters to prophesy regarding God's plan, characters respond with praise when God's activity is discerned, and God's plan is expressed through language such as "the will/purpose of God" and divine necessity. But Luke never gives us a propositional definition of who this God is, nor does he offer us a set of character attributes.[2]

What can we say about the identity of the God of Acts? Each of the five descriptions of God listed below will be expanded upon throughout the rest of our study, but these should provide us with some helpful orientation to the centrality of God within the book of Acts.

1. Portions of this chapter have been reproduced and revised from Jipp, "Beginnings of a Theology."

2. Helpful here is Gaventa, *Acts*, 28–39.

(1) GOD HAS ELECTED ISRAEL AS HIS PEOPLE

Readers of Acts must recognize that the God of Acts is *Israel's* God. The story of the rise of the church as a multi-ethnic people composed of Jews and non-Jews takes place as part of God's covenant dealings with his people Israel. Thus, Paul designates God as "the God of this people Israel who has elected our fathers" (13:17a). Paul's object of worship is "the God of my ancestors" (24:14). Peter speaks of God as "the God of Abraham, Isaac, and Jacob, the God of our ancestors" (3:13a). Stephen proclaims God to be "the God of your ancestors, the God of Abraham, of Isaac, and of Jacob" (7:32; cf. 7:46). Luke's narrations of God's actions are consistently situated within God's dealings with Israel's "fathers/ancestors" (3:25; 4:25; 5:30; 7:11–52; 13:17–36; 15:10; 22:14; 26:6; 28:25).

It is worth noting that for Luke the only people who have a history worth retelling is Israel.[3] Up until the recent events of God's sending Jesus, God had allowed "all the nations to go their own way" (Acts 14:16); God had "overlooked the times of ignorance" of the rest of the nations, and *now* commands people to turn to Jesus (17:30–31). As Jacob Jervell has said, "The God well known to Israel is wholly unknown to the Gentiles, and so their history is a story of ignorance and idolatry."[4] Israel, however, has a specific history marked by God's active involvement. This comes out in two speeches in particular that situate the work of Messiah Jesus within God's election of his people of Israel. In Acts 7 charges are brought against Stephen, one of the Hellenistic Jewish believers in Jesus, from the Sanhedrin. Stephen is essentially accused of apostasy—he speaks against the temple, the Law, and Moses (6:11–15).

---

3. This is a point frequently noted by Jacob Jervell.
4. Jervell, *Theology of the Acts*, 24.

In response, Stephen presents a complicated retelling of the history of Israel that emphasizes God's faithfulness to give Israel faithful rulers, primarily Moses, even amidst Israel's idolatry and faithlessness. Stephen's speech is full of criticism of Israel for idolatry and for the refusal to listen to the leaders that God has raised up for his people, but nowhere is there a hint that God has turned away from his people.

In Acts 13 Paul is invited to give a "word of exhortation" in the synagogue (13:15). Paul begins his sermon by presenting a mini-history of God's people, whereby he emphasizes God as beneficently electing and caring for the people Israel. God is the subject of ten verbs in 13:17–23 wherein he is portrayed as compassionately leading his own people out of Egypt (v. 17), nourishing them in the wilderness (v. 18), giving them land for an inheritance (v. 19), and granting them judges and prophets (v. 20). Paul's sermon is driving toward God's act of fulfilling the promises made to David through raising Jesus the Messiah from the dead, but it is critical for Luke that Jesus is situated within Israel's history. The story of the Messiah is not, then, something separated from Israel's history but is of one piece with God's covenant dealings with his people.

(2) GOD HAS ACTED IN AND THROUGH MESSIAH JESUS

Of course, as important as God's election of Israel and his faithfulness to his people is for the book of Acts, Luke's attention is occupied by what God has done for his people in the recent events of Jesus of Nazareth. Jesus is the Messiah of Israel, the one who rules from heaven over Israel and grants covenantal blessings of forgiveness, peace, and salvation (e.g., Acts 13:34–41). Jesus is the rejected prophet like Moses (3:22–23; 7:17–37), God's servant (3:13, 26; 4:25,

27, 30), the ruler and Savior (3:15; 5:31), and Lord (2:36; 10:36). If Luke's first volume was about "all that Jesus *began to do and teach*" (1:1), in many ways the book of Acts can be seen as providing a window into what the risen and ascended Jesus *continues* to do from his heavenly location.[5] This Jesus, Peter declares to his audience, "was a man attested to you by God with miracles, wonders, and signs that God did among you" (2:24). The consistent refrain throughout the speeches in Acts is that "you crucified Jesus of Nazareth" but "*God* has raised him up" (e.g., 2:23–24; 3:13–15; 5:30–32). Again, "God has raised this Jesus; we are all witnesses of this" (2:33). Therefore, God's bestowal of the Spirit is sent by way of Messiah Jesus (2:33–35). God continues to grant healings through Jesus (3:1–10; 4:8–12; 14:8–10). God will righteously judge the entire world at his appointed time through Jesus (17:31). I will return to this theme in more detail below (5.a.), but the point for now is clearly stated by Beverly Gaventa who notes that "one cannot any longer speak of God without reference to God's action in Jesus Christ."[6]

(3) THE GOD OF ISRAEL IS THE ONE TRUE GOD

The claim that God is the one true God is really an extension of our first point that the God of Acts *is* the God of Israel. One of the most basic confessions of Israel is known as the *Shema* and is inscribed in Deut 6:4: "Listen, Israel: The Lord our God, the Lord is one." This statement about God is less a philosophical articulation of monotheism as it is a call to Israel to show love and exclusive allegiance to the one God, and this is why the next verse declares: "You

5. On this theme in Acts I have learned much from Sleeman, *Geography and the Ascension*.

6. Gaventa, *Acts*, 29.

shall love the Lord your God with all your heart, with all your soul, and with all your strength" (Deut 6:5). The book of Acts, likewise, is clear that the God of Israel and Jesus Christ is the only true God. We will look at these episodes in more detail in the following chapters, so I will be brief in making this point now. But the power of God at work in the apostles and witnesses brooks no competitors and is superior in every way to wonder-workers and hubristic tyrants (8:14–24; 12:20–23; 13:4–12). When the Lystrans encounter Paul's healing of a lame man, they shout, "The gods have come down to us in human form" (14:11b) and attempt to offer sacrifices to them (14:13). Paul responds by referring to their religious polytheistic impulses as "worthless" and calls them to turn to the (singular) "living God" (14:15). Paul's clearest articulation of this point is found in his speech among the Hellenistic philosophers where he argues that it is the God who raised Jesus from the dead who alone is responsible for the creation of the world, who made humanity, and who providentially and beneficently sustains creation (17:22–31).

(4) GOD GUIDES AND PROTECTS THE CHURCH

One of the great questions, if not *the* fundamental question, of the history of early Christianity concerns how a tiny group of worshippers of a crucified Jew was transformed into a worldwide movement that is still with us today.[7] The book of Acts has a contribution to make to this question; namely, God is the one responsible for the church's existence *and* for its continued growth. Throughout Acts there are enemies and threats that stand against God's people and seek to damage them, compromise their unity, and ultimately eradicate their existence. The church faces

7. For one influential account, see Stark, *Rise of Christianity*.

seemingly insurmountable barriers standing against both its existence *and* its movement into new territories and regions, but God's sovereign plan for the church cannot be stopped.

Let's take an extended look at how God protects his people from a surprising enemy—Judas, Jesus's former disciple. Luke characterizes Judas as an enemy of the Messiah and the Messiah's people in a variety of ways. In the Gospel, Luke says that "Satan entered into Judas the one called Iscariot" (Luke 22:3). The narrator's note that Judas "was looking for the right time to hand over" Jesus to the authorities (22:6) eerily reminds the reader that the devil departed from Jesus after his failed attempts to tempt Jesus but only "until another time" (4:13b). Judas's conspiracy against Jesus demonstrates that he has aligned himself, as Jesus declares, with "the authority of darkness" (22:53b).

It is no small detail that Luke draws attention to greed for money as the motivating factor in Judas's treachery, for Luke's antagonists almost invariably make wrong use of possessions and money (e.g., Luke 20:45–47; Acts 5:1–11; 8:18–23; 16:16–18). So too Judas leaves behind his ministry in order to "acquire a field as the reward for his unrighteousness" (1:18a). Peter's statement that Judas left his ministry "in order to go to his own place" (1:25b) on one level simply describes his decision to abandon his ministry for the sake of acquiring his land and property. But his decision to "go to his own place" also results in his horrible death on his land. As Johnson says, "Judas's apostasy from the Twelve is expressed by the buying of a farm, his perdition is expressed by the desertion of the property, that empty property expresses the vacancy in the apostolic circle."[8]

Judas is also characterized as an enemy of the Messiah through Peter's use of two Davidic Psalms that anticipate

8. Johnson, *Acts of the Apostles*, 40; also see Parsons, *Acts*, 33–34.

Judas's treachery (Ps 69:26 in Acts 1:20a; Ps 109:8 in Acts 1:20b). Peter's claim that Judas's act was in some way "a necessity" (1:21), without providing reason or motive for his act of betrayal, again points to the Psalms' depiction of the suffering righteous king. Luke melds together Ps 69:25 (LXX 68:26) and Ps 109:8 (LXX 108:8) to describe Judas's fate as an enemy of the suffering king. Psalm 69 portrays a suffering righteous king, God's own servant (v. 17), unjustly persecuted by his own enemies (vv. 1–4, 19–29) and crying out to God for vindication (vv. 1–2, 30–36). Likewise, the Davidic Psalm 109 describes the persecution of the righteous king whereby he prays for curses against his enemies. The Psalm ends with David's words of praise to God as the one who vindicates his "servant" (LXX 108:28), who stands at the "right hand" (v. 31) of those unjustly persecuted, and gives retribution to the wicked (vv. 28–31).[9] We will have much more to say about Luke's use of the Psalms in due course, but here I simply want to draw attention to the way in which Judas is playing the part of the enemy of the royal psalmist who cries out to God for help from his violent and wicked persecutors.

All of these factors work together to depict Judas as an enemy of Jesus, the Lord's Anointed, and explain Peter's descriptive and graphic retelling of Judas's death not for the purpose of gloating in the downfall of his enemies but, rather, as an encouragement and warning that God will protect the church. Peter announces that Judas's death "became known to everyone who lived in Jerusalem" (1:19a) as an implicit warning about how God responds to those who threaten the messianic movement. While Gamaliel has not yet voiced his warning to the Sanhedrin to leave the community alone "lest you be found to be a God-fighter" (5:40),

9. I have written on this in more detail in Jipp, "Luke's Scriptural Suffering Messiah," 266–69.

Judas is the first of a handful of figures who receive divine retribution for their violence against the Messiah and his people—an act that Luke's narrative holds to be fighting against God.[10]

Our extended look at Judas provides a preview of how God responds to continued threats against the church. The threats made against the disciples from the Jewish Sanhedrin are demonstrated to be futile when, in response to their prayer to continue to speak boldly even amidst the persecution and suffering they are experiencing, God responds, "When they had prayed, the place where they were assembled was shaken, and they were all filled with the Holy Spirit and began to speak the word of God boldly" (4:31). God's commitment to the gospel taking root in Jerusalem is forceful and obvious when, in response to the apostles's arrest by the high priest and Sadducees, God sends an angel of the Lord to release them from prison *in order to go back to the temple in order to continue their testimony* (5:19–20).

Perhaps the most surprising event whereby God protects his church from its enemies occurs when the risen Christ encounters Saul in Acts 9. Most have been taught to think of this episode as narrating Saul's *conversion*, and there is certainly some truth in this. But we should recognize that Saul is characterized as an enemy of God who has given his life to eradicating the church.[11] He is present and in agreement with those who put Stephen to death (8:1). Luke speaks of Paul as "ravaging the church" and going from "house to house [to] drag off men and women and put them in prison" (8:3). He is "breathing threats and murder against the disciples of the Lord" (9:2). Thus, God's response to Saul's activity is full of irony as God defeats and

10. Shauf, *Divine in Acts*, 238.

11. On Acts 9 as narrating God's overthrow or defeat of an enemy, see especially Gaventa, *From Darkness to Light*.

overthrows this enemy of the church and transforms him into his star witness, God's "chosen instrument to take [the Lord's] name to Gentiles, kings, and Israelites" (9:15). And after spending some time with the disciples in Damascus, Paul immediately begins to proclaim in the Jewish synagogues that Jesus is the Messiah, the Son of God (9:20–22).

God is active not only to protect the church but also to ensure that the church grows and extends into new geographical territories. We have seen this briefly already in the note about Saul's divine commission to take the Lord's name to the Gentiles (9:15), and we will examine it again in the Peter-Cornelius episode in a moment. But here I want to take a look at two episodes where God moves the mission of the church forward into new geographical territories. First, Luke describes the church in Antioch as composed of a diverse group of prophets, teachers, and worshippers. During their time of worship the church hears the Holy Spirit declare, "Set apart for me Barnabas and Saul for the work to which I have called them" (13:2). The "work" God has prepared for Barnabas and Saul is narrated in their missionary endeavors (often referred to as Paul's first missionary journey) in Cyprus and Asia Minor (narrated in Acts 13:4—14:28). God directs Paul's travels in another surprising way in Acts 16, where Paul and his team's plans are at first frustrated when the Holy Spirit forbids them to work in Asia (16:6) and then again, the Spirit of Jesus prevents them from missionary work in Mysia (16:7). Carl Holladay is on the mark when he says that by "describing the itinerary as a zigzag pattern . . . Luke emphasizes that the travel plans of the missionaries are divinely directed rather than humanly planned."[12] While they are waiting in Troas, Paul receives a vision of a Macedonian man who is pleading with Paul to "cross over into Macedonia and help us!" (16:9b).

12. Holladay, *Acts*, 317.

Paul and his team draw the conclusion that "God had called us to preach the gospel to them" (16:10). In this way, the message of Jesus Christ moves further westward as it goes across the Bosphorus and into Greece.

(5) GOD'S ACTIVITY REQUIRES HUMAN DISCERNMENT AND INTERPRETATION

One of the most surprising facets of God's activity in Acts is that God's acts and plans are rarely obvious to characters within the narrative.[13] God and his purposes are frequently misunderstood; human "ignorance" of God and his purposes is at the heart of the story's conflicts; when God's activity *is* recognized it is frequently a lengthy and painful process for the characters; God's purposes remain hidden to most and are often rejected. And yet God's plans are accomplished *through* human participation in his purposes and response to his acts. Especially in Acts one finds God's purposes come to fruition only when the church rightly interprets and aligns itself with what God has done. Acts is, in fact, all about how God's plan is "willed, initiated, impelled, and guided by God through the Holy Spirit."[14] Despite this, however, the narrator rarely *directly* refers to God doing something, and never does God appear directly and obviously.[15] Rather, identifying, naming, and interpreting God's work in the world is usually left to the characters who are responsible to discern God's activity through various media. The narrator speaks of many events such as healings and exorcisms, prison escapes, ecstatic speech, and visions. But Luke's tendency is to have the characters discern that

13. This section contains overlap with my more extensive argument in Jipp, "Beginnings of a Theology," 23–43.

14. Johnson, *Acts of the Apostles*, 15.

15. Marguerat, *First Christian Historian*, 86–92.

God is the one acting through these events and to have them interpret their theological significance.

Divine activity is, then, never obvious, often ambiguous, and, hence, mandates human interpretation. Luke's account of divine action intersects the fabric of human lives as to respect the importance of human decisions and preserve God's transcendence. Thus, within Acts one finds an interplay between event and interpretation, that is, between God's interventions in history *and* the characters directly naming God. Acts not only recounts God's acts within history but it does so in order to teach its readers to discern, interpret, and testify to God's continuing work.[16] The reader who identifies with the apostles' interpretation of God's acts learns how to respond to divine activity in her own world. Allow me to demonstrate this with three examples.

(a) God and the Death and Resurrection of Jesus

Within the Gospel of Luke there are no explicit references to *God* willing Jesus's death or to his act of raising him from the dead. Quite simply, "God" is never the explicit subject of any statement regarding Jesus's death and resurrection in the Gospel. The reader does ascertain, however implicitly, that the events of the Passion belong to God's plan. But while it may be clear to the reader familiar with Luke's narrative, the indications that Jesus's death is the will of God remain implicit. So, for example, the relation between God's plan and Jesus's death is hinted at through the use of language like "it is necessary/must" (Luke 9:22; 13:33; 17:25; 22:37), through ambiguous divine passives (5:35; 9:44; 18:32; 22:37), through the testimony of the Scriptures (18:31; 20:17; 22:37), and through the comment that Jesus was discussing "his exodus which was about to be fulfilled

16. Marguerat, *First Christian Historian*, 91.

in Jerusalem" (9:31). Not once is God named as the initiator of the events of the Passion in Luke 22–23, and there are no direct references to divine activity within these chapters.[17] The overwhelming sense of these chapters, in fact, is that the active agents in Jesus's death are Satan and Jesus's human enemies (22:2, 3, 31, 48, 53).[18] And, in fact, often it is "the will" or "the plan" of Jesus's opponents initiating Jesus's sufferings that is emphasized (e.g., 23:25, 51). One may *infer* that God's refusal to answer Jesus's prayer—"Father, if you are willing, take this cup from me, but not my will but yours be done" (22:42)—is an indication that Jesus's death is God's will, but it is not yet obviously so. Again, Jesus foretells the *necessity* of his resurrection, but its relation to divine activity is not explicit (9:22; cf. 24:26, 44). Jesus declares that "he will rise up on the third day" (18:33) as part of the "fulfillment of all the things written by the prophets about the Son of Man" (18:31b), but God is not mentioned directly. And even the angels' use of the passive in their response to the women—"he has been raised" (24:6)—does not state that *God* has raised Jesus. Despite hints, there are, then, no direct unambiguous statements regarding God's role in Jesus's death and resurrection in the Gospel.

There is a distinct shift in the theological discourse in Acts when the apostles directly refer to Jesus's death and resurrection as the result of God's activity.[19] Peter's statements that Jesus's death was the result of "God's determined will and foreknowledge" (2:23), that "God has fulfilled all he foretold through the mouth of all the prophets regarding the suffering of his Christ" (3:18), and that Jesus's enemies in crucifying him accomplished all "your hand and will had

17. Note Squires, *Plan of God*, 56.

18. See Frei, *Identity of Jesus Christ*, 121.

19. On this aspect of Luke's theological discourse, see Mowery, "Lord, God, and Father."

determined" (4:28), declare explicitly what the Gospel had only indicated implicitly. The statements regarding God's agency in raising Jesus from the dead are even more explicit when the apostles make numerous statements where "God" is the subject, followed by a verb for resurrection, and Jesus as the object: "God raised him" (2:24), "God raised this Jesus" (2:32), "God raised him from the dead" (4:10), "God raised him on the third day" (10:40; cf. 3:15; 5:30; 13:30, 33, 34, 37; 17:31).

By withholding direct acknowledgment of God's activity in the events surrounding Jesus's death and resurrection, Luke moves the reader from the event to its interpretation, from apparent human activity in the passion narrative to its theological meaning. The apostles are portrayed, then, as moving from ignorance to discernment, interpretation, and testimony. How does Luke narrate the apostles' transition from the implicit to the explicit, or, in this case, from misunderstanding God's plan to being faithful witnesses and interpreters of it? First, the apostles have *aligned themselves with Jesus's understanding of God's plan.* Jesus's declarations regarding the necessity of his sufferings, death, and resurrection have been internalized by the witnesses and are now proclaimed directly. Second, the witnesses have undergone a *transformation in their ability to read Israel's Scriptures* as finding their fulfillment in the Messiah's death and resurrection (Acts 2:24–35; 4:10–11, 25–28; cf. Luke 24:24–27, 44–49). Third, the outpouring of the Spirit has empowered them to interpret and testify to God's acts (Luke 24:48–49; Acts 2:33–35). And fourth, their experience of the empty tomb and the living Christ has enabled them to see the events of the passion as divine activity (Luke 24:8–12, 28–35, 36–43; Acts 1:1–8).

(b) God and Scripture

One of the primary ways that humans discern the ways of God is through the interpretation of Israel's sacred Scriptures. For example, Peter interprets the event whereby the Jews in Jerusalem are empowered to speak in different languages and dialects as the fulfillment of God's promise in Joel 3 (LXX), namely, as the outpouring of God's prophetic spirit on his people (2:1–13; 2:17–21). James, later the leader of the Jerusalem church, interprets the inclusion of non-Jews within God's people as in "harmony with the words of the prophets" (15:15–18). And Paul draws upon Isaiah's prophetic oracle of warning and judgment as a means of explaining continued Jewish unbelief in Jesus as the Messiah (28:25–28; cf. Isa 6:9).

We have already had occasion to look at the Judas episode in Acts 1:15–26 from the standpoint of God's protection of his people from their enemies. Let's look at the text again to see the way in which Peter engages in the interpretation of Israel's Scriptures as a means of making sense of Judas's apostasy and subsequent gory demise. Peter's ability to discern the work of God through Israel's Scriptures here is remarkable when one remembers his inability to understand Jesus's statements regarding the *necessity* of the Messiah's death and resurrection in Luke's Gospel (see Luke 9:21–22; 9:44–45; 18:31–34). Peter's initial words—"it was necessary for the Scripture to be fulfilled" (Acts 1:16a)—portray Peter now as a reliable interpreter of the relationship between divine activity and Israel's Scriptures. Again, in verse 21 Peter's understanding of Israel's Scriptures (1:20) enables him to see the "necessity" of finding a replacement for Judas. Whereas in Luke's Gospel it was primarily Jesus and the narrator who understood the plan of God and its providential workings, a hermeneutical transformation has taken place with respect to Peter that enables him to reliably interpret God's workings.[20] Furthermore, Peter's claim in 1:16 makes a strong connection to some of Jesus's final words where he declares to his disciples, "These are my words which I spoke to you while I was still with you *that it is necessary for everything about me written in the law of Moses, the prophets, and the psalms must be fulfilled*" (Luke 24:44; cf. 24:26–27). Peter takes up, then, the hermeneutical commission of the risen Jesus as they interpret and make sense of God's ongoing activity through reference to the pattern of scriptural interpretation set in motion by Jesus. This is indeed a remarkable paradigm shift in the characterization of Peter and the apostles who, I would suggest, continue the ministry of Jesus through their discernment of God's ongoing work. One also sees here the literary fulfillment of Jesus's promise that after Peter's betrayal of Jesus, Peter would be restored in order to edify and establish his fellow brothers (Luke 22:31–32).[21]

The contemporary interpreter should also recognize that Peter's actual interpretation of Scripture is not haphazard or careless. We have already noted that he draws upon two Davidic Psalms and explicitly says that these writings were spoken "*through the mouth of David about Judas* who became a guide to those who arrested Jesus" (1:16b). We will continue to see the importance of the Psalms as Lukan messianic intertexts (see especially Acts 2:22–36), but here we should simply note that Peter sees the Psalms' pattern of the wicked persecutors of the righteous Davidic king as having its referent in the events of Jesus's suffering, death, and resurrection. God's vindication of his anointed often comes through judgment, hence Peter's picking up on the

20. On the motif and vocabulary of providence in Luke-Acts, see Squires, *Plan of God*.

21. Parsons, *Acts*, 32.

Psalmist's prayer: "let his dwelling place become desolate and let no love live in it" (Acts 1:20a).

(c) God, Angels, Dreams, and Visions

Humans in Acts often discern the work of God by means of angelic messengers, dreams, and visions. This is no surprise, given Peter's programmatic quotation about the work of the Spirit from Joel 3: "and it shall be in the last days, says God, I will pour out my Spirit upon all people and your sons and daughters will prophesy and your young men *will see visions* and your old men *will dream dreams* (2:17)." Thus, Saul is transformed from enemy into pastor and missionary by a vision of Christ, a vision which is explained for him by Ananias (9:1–19). God sends Cornelius an angelic messenger and commands him to send for Peter (10:1–8); Peter, simultaneously, receives a vision from heaven telling him that God has cleansed the Gentiles (10:9–16). Paul the prisoner receives an angelic messenger who informs him that he will make it safely to Rome in order to appear before Caesar and that they will first shipwreck on an island (27:21–26).

REFLECTIONS

1. In this chapter, I suggest that God is revealed through the story Acts tells us. What are the benefits and challenges of seeing God's identity revealed through narrative rather than through propositional statements or attribute descriptions?

2. What might be some of the implications of God's acting within the narrative of Acts for the earliest readers' concrete situation? Does Acts intend for the story of God to end at the close of this narrative?

3

ISRAEL'S RESTORATION AND THE MESSIAH'S RESURRECTION

IF THE GOD OF Acts is the God who has chosen to enter into a covenant relationship with Israel his people, as we saw in the previous chapter, then we might rightly wonder about the relationship between Israel and the church as it is recounted in Acts. Has the church subsumed or replaced Israel? Has God bypassed the promises he made to Israel or perhaps pushed them off into the far off distant future? Does Luke's celebration of the mission to the Gentiles come at the expense of Israel? Answering these questions is no theoretical matter, for the way in which Luke answers these questions will determine whether or not this God of Israel is faithful to his promises and whether he can be trusted to keep his word.

(1) THE GOSPEL OF LUKE ANTICIPATES GOD'S FULFILLMENT OF HIS PROMISES TO ISRAEL

The Gospel of Luke begins with expectations that God is doing something great for his people Israel. In particular, the infancy narrative (Luke 1–2) primes the reader's expectations for how to read the rest of the Gospel of Luke *as well as* the book of Acts. And in particular, it leads the reader to interpret Luke's story of Jesus in full continuity with God's dealings with Israel in the Hebrew Scriptures. Let's look briefly at a few of these themes.

(a) Israel's Barren Women

God's miraculous opening of the womb of the barren and elderly Elizabeth (1:5–25) and the Spirit's impregnation of Mary (1:34–38) recall the stories of the barren women in Israel's Scriptures such as Sarah (Gen 18:9–15) and Hannah (1 Sam 1–2). God's opening of the wombs of these barren women functioned to mark new beginnings in God's relations with his people, namely, the fulfillment of God's covenant with Abraham and the rise of Israel's monarchy. Here too God's supernatural dealings with Elizabeth and Mary indicate God's active presence among his people again.[1]

(b) A Davidic King to Rule Israel Forever

One of the primary promises in Israel's Scriptures was that God would maintain his loyal love to his servant King David by ensuring that one of his offspring/seed would sit on David's throne ruling over God's people (e.g., 2 Sam 7:12–14; 1 Chr 17; Pss 2, 89; cf. Gen 49:8–12). It is of obvious significance, then, that the son born to Mary is a Davidite (2:4). The angel Gabriel announces to Mary that the child to be born to her "will be great and will be called the Son of the Most High, and the Lord God will give him the throne of his father David. He will reign over the house of Jacob forever, and his kingdom will have no end" (Luke 1:32–33). Similarly, the angels report to the shepherds the good news

1. See here especially Green, "Problem of a Beginning." More broadly, see González, *Story Luke Tells*, 15–18.

that "today in the city of David a Savior has been born for you; he is *the Messiah*, the Lord" (2:11).

(c) Promises to Abraham

The bulk of Genesis, the first book of the Bible, is dominated by God's promises to Abraham and their outworking in Abraham's family. God promises to make Abraham into a great nation, to give him land and a worldwide family, and to bless the nations through him (Gen 12:1–4). Thus, the reader takes note when Mary responds to God's promise to grant her a son with a hymn, in particular a hymn that declares, "He [i.e., God] has helped his servant Israel, remembering his mercy to Abraham and his seed forever, just as he spoke to our ancestors" (Luke 1:54–55). And Zechariah, similarly, declares, "He has dealt mercifully with our fathers and remembered his holy covenant, the oath that he swore to our father Abraham" (1:72–73).

(d) Israel's Restoration and the Prophetic Spirit

Luke's Infancy Narrative contains two vignettes of aged prophets who prophesy over Jesus. Simeon was an old and righteous Jerusalemite who had been "anticipating Israel's consolation" (2:25). God had told him that he would live to see the birth of the Messiah. When Jesus is brought into the temple, Simeon is filled with the Spirit and proclaims, "My eyes have seen your salvation. You have prepared it in the presence of all peoples, a light for revelation to the Gentiles and glory to your people Israel" (2:31–32). Furthermore, he declares that the coming of Jesus will mean both the "fall and rise of many in Israel and a sign that will be opposed . . . that the thoughts of many hearts may be revealed" (2:34). Then Anna, another righteous and godly prophetess, sees

Jesus and begins to "give thanks to God and to speak about him to all who were looking forward to the redemption of Jerusalem" (2:38). The Holy Spirit who empowers prophetic utterances is here in full measure upon these prophets (cf. also Elizabeth in 1:41–45 and Zechariah in 1:67–79), and they interpret the coming of Jesus as good news for everyone who is hoping and praying for God's restoration of Israel.

(2) ACTS 1:1–8 CONNECTS THE PLOT WITH GOD'S PROMISE TO FULFILL HIS PROMISES TO ISRAEL

Of course, the Gospel of Luke does not narrate God's restoration of Israel in a conflict-free manner. The majority of Israel's leaders, both the Pharisees as well as the Jerusalem priestly leaders, do not embrace Jesus as the Messiah. The Pharisees rebuke the disciples for praising their King as he makes his way into Jerusalem (Luke 19:38–40). Jesus weeps for Jerusalem and laments for her continued waywardness from God's purposes (19:41–44). And ultimately, of course, Jesus is crucified at the behest of Israel's chief priests (22:1–2, 66–71). But has Israel's leaders' rejection of Jesus disqualified Israel as God's people? Have God's promises and the joyful and hopeful expectations of Luke's infancy narrative become null and void due to their unbelief?

When the disciples ask Jesus in Acts 1:6 if he will now restore the kingdom to Israel, many have assumed that the disciples are asking an obtuse, wrong-headed question. But even our initial foray into Luke 1–2 would suggest that this theme is close to the heart of Luke's Gospel. Are the disciples who have now spent forty days with the risen Jesus really so off target as that? Let's take a look at the introduction of Acts to see how Acts 1:1–11 functions as the prologue to the book *and* how it connects Acts to the God who is committed to his people Israel.

Luke summarizes the content of the risen Jesus's forty-day proclamation to his disciples with the familiar language of "*the kingdom of God*" (1:3b). The disciples, too, question Jesus about the timing of the restoration of "*the kingdom to Israel*" (1:6b). And the language of God's kingdom will occur at important moments within the narrative in order to summarize the content of the proclamation of Christ's witnesses (see Acts 8:12; 14:22; 19:8; 20:25; 28:23, 31). Most readers will also remember that Luke's Jesus repeatedly spoke of God's kingdom (e.g., Luke 4:43; 6:20; 8:10; 9:2, 11, 27). And Acts will soon use royal language to portray the resurrected and exalted Messiah as Israel's king (e.g., 2:30–36). This suggests that readers of Acts are intended to understand the content of the book as narrating "what the kingdom of God looks like now that Jesus has come, announced the arrival of the kingdom, died, risen and ascended to the right hand of the Father."[2] Luke connects Jesus's proclamation of God's kingdom (Acts 1:3b) to his command to stay in Jerusalem and "to wait for the promise of the Father which you heard from me" (1:4b). The language recalls Luke 24:49 where Jesus declares that *he* will send the promise *of the Father* in order to clothe his witnesses with heavenly power. What Jesus *sends* and what the Father has *promised* is explicitly spoken of in 1:5b and 1:8a, namely, the Holy Spirit who will empower the witnesses for mission.

The twin motifs of God's kingdom and Spirit understandably lead to the concern with the role of Israel in God's purposes, as the disciples ask, "Lord, is it at this time that you will restore the kingdom to Israel?" (1:6). This is an

2. Thompson, *Acts of the Risen Lord Jesus*, 47. Thompson's entire discussion on this matter is excellent and worth consulting.

understandable and entirely appropriate question, given that many of Israel's prophetic Scriptures anticipate a day when God will act to restore the fortunes of God's people by sending the Spirit. While Israel's writings present different versions of what this will look like, the outpouring of the Holy Spirit is frequently associated with a new act of God to restore, refresh, and empower God's people (e.g., Isa 32:15; 44:3; Ezek 36:27; 37:14; Joel 2:28–29). Luke's language in 1:8, in fact, seems to recall Isa 32:15, where Israel's desolation is reversed when the "Spirit from on high is poured out on us."[3] Later, in fact, Peter exhorts the people to repent so that they might experience "times of refreshment from the face of the Lord" (3:19–20). These times of refreshment come from the heavenly figure (3:21) who grants signs of his favor, presence, and healing to those who turn to him as a foretaste of his "time of universal restoration" (3:21a). The parallels between 3:20–21 and 1:6–11 (times and seasons, restoration, heaven, Jesus's return, Spirit/refreshment) suggest that the heavenly enthroned king is actively responsible for pouring out blessings upon his repentant people in anticipation of his return.[4]

Further, while Jesus's words in 1:7–8 have often been read as entirely unrelated to the disciples' question in 1:6, Jesus does actually speak directly of Israel in his response. The map for the mission of the witnesses functions as more than a geographical outline of the disciples' travels. Rather, the Spirit-empowered witnesses of the enthroned Davidic Messiah are told that they will provide their testimony in Jerusalem—the city of David, Zion, and home to the temple and its leaders. The theological importance of Jerusalem at this point in the narrative could not be stronger, as Luke has consistently spoken of the city as the place where God's

3. See Pao, *Acts*, 132–34.

4. Anderson, *"But God Raised Him"*, 228.

promises and salvation will be on display (e.g., Luke 2:38; 9:31, 51, 53; 13:33–35; 18:34; 19:11; 24:47). In addition to Jerusalem, the witnesses will testify *not* to "Judea, and then Samaria," but to "all Judea *and* Samaria," thereby recalling the prophetic anticipations of a return to a united Israel where both the northern and southern kingdoms are reconciled and at peace with each other (e.g., Ezek 37). The witnesses will even go "until the end of the earth," a geographical marker that also appears in Acts 13:47 and its quotation of Isa 49:6—"I have appointed you for a light to the nations to bring salvation to the end of the earth." Both within Acts 13 and Isa 49 the phrase "the end of the earth" refers to Gentiles, but within its Isaianic context the salvation of the Gentiles is dependent upon the prior restoration of Israel through God's Servant (Isa 49:5–6).[5] These factors suggest that with Jesus's proclamation of God's kingdom, the anticipation of the promised Spirit of Israel's prophets, and the apostles' witness to Israel, Jesus does not deny Israel's restoration. Jesus does not push the restoration into the indefinite future, nor does he rebuke the disciples for their misplaced concern about "*national*" Israel. If Luke intends for the reader to view the disciples as rubes for asking about Israel's restoration, then Luke's own emphasis on God's kingdom, the Spirit, the distinctly Israelite geographical language in 1:8, and the emphasis on Jesus as Israel's enthroned Davidic Messiah are inexplicable.

Verses 7–8 are theologically programmatic for the entire narrative as they define the fundamental acting roles for both God *and* the apostles. When the disciples ask Jesus whether it is at "this time" that Jesus will restore Israel's kingdom, Jesus directs their attention to the Father who alone has this power and authority to determine its timing. God

5. Pao, *Acts*, 91–95. The phrase "the end of the earth" only occurs five times in the LXX (Isa 8:9; 48:20; 49:6; 62:11; *Ps. Sol.* 1:4).

is *the* sovereign actor who sets events in motion and almost always in surprising and unpredictable ways. Whether this is the surprising event of God's pouring out the Spirit at Pentecost (2:1–13), the call and conversion of Saul (9:1–19), the inclusion of Cornelius and the Gentiles into God's family (10:1—11:18), or the movement of the mission into Macedonia (16:6–10), the rest of Acts will demonstrate the primacy of God as the one who has the power and authority to accomplish his purposes in his own timing and way.[6] The rest of the narrative is theologically governed by Jesus's words in Acts 1:8, which is one of the "central causes that drive the rest of the narrated happenings."[7] We can better understand, then, the importance of the disciples as *witnesses* (1:8). Specifically, their role is to witness and provide testimony to God's powerful activity in raising Messiah Jesus from the dead and God's outpouring of the Spirit (1:23; 2:32; 3:15; 5:32; 13:31). In other words, the missionary role of the disciples consists primarily in their proclamation of how God's power and authority has been enacted.

(3) ACTS 1–5 NARRATES GOD'S RESTORATION OF ISRAEL IN JERUSALEM

The early chapters of Acts are concerned with demonstrating how God has been faithful to the promises he made to Israel. The mission to the Gentiles has been successful and is worthy of celebration, but the salvation of the Gentiles has not come at the expense of God's faithfulness to his covenant people. Specifically, Luke shows in the early chapters of Acts that God has: a) restored Israel through the twelve disciples who symbolically represent Israel's twelve tribes; b) poured out the promised prophetic Holy Spirit; c) raised

6. See Parsons, *Acts*, 28.
7. Shauf, *Divine in Acts*, 279–80.

up a son of David to eternally rule over God's people; and d) created a faithful, repentant remnant of Jerusalemite believers.

(a) The Reconstitution of Israel's Twelve Tribes and the True Leaders of God's People

In Acts 1:15–26 Luke narrates the reconstitution of the apostles through the replacement of Judas. There is an emphasis in these verses on numbering. The list of the *eleven* apostles in verse 13 makes the absence of Judas notable. Judas was, after all, directly chosen by the Lord to be "one of the Twelve" (Luke 22:3; cf. Luke 6:14–16; Acts 1:2). Peter declares that Judas "was numbered among us" (Acts 1:17a). When Matthias is chosen, the narrator says he is "added with the eleven apostles" (1:26b).[8] That Matthias's significance lies solely in his bringing the number of the apostles to twelve is highlighted by the fact "that Matthias does not reappear in the rest of the Lukan narrative."[9] Why did Peter and the apostles consider it a necessity to replace Judas? Why does Luke highlight the theme of numbering? And what are the specific valences of the number twelve?

We have already seen that one of the primary themes of Luke *and* Acts consists in narrating God's faithfulness to act for the redemption of Israel. A few examples (Luke 1:54–55; 2:25–28) follow. When the reader of Luke's Gospel hears of the twelve baskets left from the Messiah's hospitable provision for the crowd and Jesus's promise that the apostles "will sit on thrones judging the twelve tribes of Israel" (Luke 22:30; cf. Acts 26:6–8), s/he can see that the number twelve is connected to Israel as God's restored people.[10] As Jesus

---

8. On the theme of numbering, see Pao, *Acts*, 123–29.

9. Pao, *Acts*, 123.

10. On these matters, it is hard to improve upon Jervell, "Twelve

prepares for his trial and death, he declares to *the Twelve*, "Just as the Father conferred the kingdom to me, so I am also conferring the kingdom upon you" (Luke 22:29). The Twelve will rule over the twelve tribes of Israel "*in my [the Messiah's] kingdom*" (Luke 22:30). Again, we can see that the disciples' initial question in Acts about the restoration of the kingdom to Israel is an entirely appropriate question (Acts 1:6–8). The addition of Matthias to the eleven returns the number to twelve and constitutes a claim, not that the disciples or the church replace Israel, but that these twelve constitute the nucleus of the new leadership over Israel as God's people.[11] This prepares the reader for the frequent turf wars that will take place in chapters 3–5 between the apostles and the Sanhedrin over who constitutes the legitimate leaders of Israel.

It should also be noted that the role of the apostles here is singularly set forth in their task to be a witness to Jesus. Primarily, they are to be "a witness to his resurrection" (1:22b), and we will see that the message of the apostles will indeed center upon this event. But they also must have knowledge of Jesus's comings and goings starting with John's baptism and extending until the resurrection, and so we will not be surprised to see the apostles narrating Jesus's earthly ministry in their role as the Messiah's witnesses (e.g., 2:22; 10:36–43; cf. 1:8).

(b) The Gift of the Holy Spirit

After the reconstitution of the Twelve, Luke narrates the outpouring of the Holy Spirit. This event not only fulfills the promises made by Jesus (Luke 24:49; Acts 1:4–5, 8) and John the Baptist (Luke 3:16), but it also indicates that God

---

on Israel's Thrones," 75–112.

11. See Johnson, *Acts of the Apostles*, 38.

has begun to fulfill the prophetic promises he made to Israel to redeem and restore his people by sending a Spirit from on high (e.g., Isa 32:15; 44:3; Ezek 36:27–28; 37:14). The actual narration of this event, for all of its importance, is remarkably brief, comprising only four verses in our Bible. But Luke provides some significant, albeit subtle, clues as to the meaning and significance of the event in 2:1–4. First, the temporal setting for the giving of the Spirit at the festival of Pentecost (2:1) is reminiscent of Jewish traditions that associated the festival with God's giving of the Law at Sinai (e.g., *Jubilees* 1:1; 6:17–19; 22:1–16; 1QS I, 8–II, 25; cf. Deut 16:9–12).[12] In Acts the outpouring of the Spirit is accompanied by violent sounds from heaven, a rushing wind, and tongues like fire upon the people who are assembled together in the upper room (2:2–3). And this is highly reminiscent of Moses and Israel at Sinai where thunder, lighting, smoke, and a loud sound like a trumpet accompanies God's giving of the law to Moses and the people who are assembled to meet God (Exod 19:16–18).[13] As God constituted his people through this theophany and giving of Torah at Sinai, so now God marks out his people through this new theophany that is marked by the outpouring of the Spirit. Schnabel states it well when he says this suggests that "the Holy Spirit of God . . . is in some way the Spirit of the new covenant, or, more precisely, the Spirit of the life in the renewed covenant and thus in restored Israel."[14] We can see now even more clearly why it was necessary to have *twelve* apostolic witnesses as the symbolic representation of the leaders of the restored Israel.

Peter draws upon the prophet Joel who anticipates that God's restoration of Israel will be accompanied by sending

12. VanderKam, "Festival of Weeks," 185–205.

13. Johnson, *Acts of the Apostles*, 46.

14. Schnabel, *Acts*, 113.

the Spirit for all people (Joel 2:28–32 in Acts 2:17–21). Luke's editorial addition that prefaces the Joel quotation, "and it shall be *in the last days*," is not found in Joel and it draws attention to Luke's belief that God's outpouring of the prophetic Spirit has initiated the eschatological age and the fulfillment of God's prophetic promises.[15] The quotation from Joel is programmatic for the identity and activity of those characters who have the Spirit.[16] In other words, the Spirit-empowerment of the apostles and witnesses is demonstrated throughout the rest of the narrative in that they prophesy (2:17, 18), see dreams and visions (2:17; cf. 7:55–56; 9:3–12; 10:17–19; 16:9–10), perform signs and wonders (2:19; cf. 2:43; 4:16, 22, 30; 5:12; 6:8; 8:6, 13), and proclaim salvation to all those who call upon the Lord (2:21; cf. 7:25; 15:11; 28:28). Joel's prophecy also fits Luke's purposes to declare that God's salvation is for all people, as it speaks of the Spirit poured out on "all flesh" (2:17) and indicates that "all" who call on the Lord will be saved (2:21). We are not surprised, then, when we later come to find that the Spirit is poured out upon Samaritans (8:14–17) and non-Jews (10:44–48).

(c) The Resurrection and Enthronement of the Messianic King

The outpouring of the Holy Spirit was not only prophesied by Israel's Scriptures and promised by Jesus of Nazareth, the Spirit has now come from the risen and enthroned-in-heaven Davidic King. We remember this as one of the promises made to Mary by Gabriel, namely, that her son would be God's Son who would be given the authority to

15. Pao, *Acts*, 131, who notes the occurrence of the exact phrase in Isa 2:1.

16. This point is helpfully emphasized throughout the writings of Luke Timothy Johnson.

rule over Israel eternally (Luke 1:31–35). Acts narrates how God's Son rules over Israel from his enthroned position in heaven. The Gospel of Luke concludes (Luke 24:50–53) and Acts begins (1:9–11) with Jesus's heavenly ascension. The importance of Jesus's location in heaven is already signaled to the reader through the fourfold repetition in 1:9–11 of Jesus's current location "in heaven." While Luke places great weight on God's resurrection of Jesus as the royal enthronement whereby God fulfills his promises to David, without the narration of Jesus's heavenly ascent the reader could potentially fail to understand how the resurrected Messiah continues his work as Israel's enthroned king in heaven. It is at the ascension that God completes the process of exalting his son by enthroning him to a position of heavenly rule from where the messianic king reigns over his people, judges his enemies, and extends the sphere of his dominion. As such, Luke's depiction of Jesus's ascension as the event whereby the Messiah enters into his heavenly rule has literary significance beyond the description of the actual event, as Jesus is seen as *continuing* to enact his kingship and establishing God's kingdom from heaven.

In Acts 2:22–36 Peter engages in a highly complex interpretation of the Psalter in order to interpret Jesus's resurrection and ascension as his heavenly installation as the enthroned Davidic king *whose enthronement is the cause of the outpouring of the Spirit*. We have already seen Luke highlight Jesus as the agent who sends the Spirit (Luke 24:49; 1:4–5), but it is here that Luke shows how Jesus's resurrection and ascension is the necessary cause of the outpouring of the Spirit.[17]

Peter's speech immediately draws upon Israel's Psalter to demonstrate the inability of death to keep Jesus

17. I have reproduced and summarized a longer argument I made in Jipp, "'For David Did Not Ascend,'" 46–50.

underneath its power (2:24b) when it refers to God as the one who "raised [Jesus] *by loosing the pangs of death*" (2:24a; cf. Ps 17). Peter declares that while David is the *speaker* of the Psalms, David is not their referent or subject matter; rather, David spoke in the Psalms as a prophet (2:30) who looked forward to the Messiah's resurrection and exaltation *into* heaven (2:31–33).[18] Peter justifies this reading by exploiting the fact that David is dead, buried, and his tomb is accessible to the public in Jerusalem (2:29), but the Psalms, specifically Ps 15 (LXX), speak of a figure who is always joyfully living in God's presence, whose body will not experience decay, who will never be abandoned to Hades, and who continues to experience the ways of life.

Thus, in Acts 2:31b Peter declares that it is the resurrected Messiah who is the referent of Ps 15:9–10 (LXX) and who "has neither been abandoned into Hades nor has his flesh seen corruption." Peter's most creative interpretive move in his sermon—though one that is common in early Christian discourse—is his interpretation of the Messiah's resurrection from the dead *with* the fulfillment of God's promise to David: "God swore an oath to him [i.e., David] to seat on his throne one from the fruit of his loins" (Ps 132:11; cf. Acts 13:23; Heb 1:5). Luke's association of the Messiah's resurrection with his heavenly enthronement (see the use of Ps 131:11 and 109:1 LXX) indicates "that the enthronement at God's right hand is understood by Luke as the fulfillment of God's promise to David to seat one of his descendants upon his throne."[19] Standing behind Ps 131:11 (LXX) is God's promise to David in 2 Sam 7:12: "I will raise up after you your seed, who will come from your body,

18. For the way in which Acts and other Second Temple Jewish sources depict David as a prophetic figure, see Fitzmyer, "David," 332–39.

19. Strauss, *Davidic Messiah*, 139.

and I will establish his kingdom." Jesus's resurrection, then, must be *more than* a return to mortal existence given Peter's declaration that the Davidic Messiah now reigns over God's kingdom and shares God's heavenly throne.[20]

Psalm 15 (LXX) suits Peter's purposes nicely as it also speaks of this royal figure as one who is *located at God's right hand* (2:25b). The spatial placement of God's throne ("God's right hand") next to the Messiah is what protects the referent of Ps 15 from being shaken, and within the context of Acts 2:22–36 this almost certainly refers to God's assistance to sovereignly rescue his messianic son from death (cf. Acts 7:54–60). Again, given that the Father has invited a second Lord to "sit at my right hand" *until* God has triumphed over all their enemies and placed them under the Lord's feet (2:35), this too cannot refer to David who "did not ascend into heaven" (2:34). Obviously, Peter's scriptural interpretation *assumes* the premise that God has raised Jesus from the dead and located him in a position of heavenly and royal power; and Peter's threefold mention of the Messiah at God's right hand draws emphasis to the heavenly *location* of the Messiah's powerful rule.

Peter's use of the Davidic Psalms functions to establish that Jesus's resurrection and ascension *are* the means whereby God enthrones his Davidic king to a position of continuing heavenly rule. Peter brings together Pss 15:11 (LXX) and 109:1 (LXX), in part because of their shared phrase "at the right hand" (Acts 2:25b and 2:34b), in order to demonstrate that the resurrected Messiah is currently enthroned in heaven and shares in God's powerful rule at his right hand (Acts 2:33). This is why David himself cannot be the referent or subject matter of his own speech—David's death made it certain that David is not the one who "ascended *into heaven*" (2:34b). This statement about David,

20. Sleeman, *Geography and the Ascension*, 101.

however, reminds the reader of another figure who *has* ascended "into heaven" (1:10–11).[21] Peter uses the language of the Psalter to make precisely this point in Acts 2:33: the Messiah "who has been exalted to God's *right hand*" is the agent and the cause of the outpouring of the Spirit. The first act of the enthroned king, in other words, is to send God's powerful Spirit as the means of expanding God's kingdom (cf. Acts 1:6–11). Peter's use of Ps 109:1 and its designation of the Messiah *also as Lord* further enables him to interpret the resurrection as Jesus's heavenly enthronement to a position of absolute lordship: "God has made him both Lord and Messiah" (Acts 2:36).[22]

By anyone's reading, Peter's scriptural interpretation is complex, so allow me to summarize what Peter is doing. First, in the Psalter David speaks of a royal figure who will not experience death and who will live in God's presence at his right hand forever. Second, David cannot be speaking about himself since he has died and the place of his tomb is common knowledge to everyone in Jerusalem. He must have been speaking, therefore, as a prophet who anticipated that God would fulfill the promises made to David by sending a future king who would sit on David's throne. Third, and this is really Peter's crucial interpretive move, David anticipates the resurrection of the Messiah. The resurrection of Christ is the event whereby God enthrones one of David's seed to a position of heavenly rule. Fourth, this event, God's resurrection and enthronement of Christ, is the cause or the prior act that results in God's pouring out of the Spirit—"therefore, having been exalted to God's right hand and receiving the promise that is the Holy Spirit, *he has poured out this which you see and hear*" (Acts 2:33).

21. Anderson, *"But God Raised Him"*, 215.

22. Strauss, *Davidic Messiah*, 144–45.

Throughout Acts, then, there is a close connection between the resurrected and enthroned Davidic King, the work of the Holy Spirit, and God's faithfulness to his people Israel. In Acts 3:1–10, for example, Peter and John heal a lame man sitting at the gate of the temple. While all of the people who observe the healing are in utter amazement at the man who is now skipping and leaping, Peter declares that the act of healing has taken place by means of "the name of Messiah Jesus of Nazareth" (3:6b; cf. 4:9–10). Peter's speech explains that it is the resurrection power of "the God of Abraham, Isaac, Jacob—the God of our ancestors," which has exalted Jesus and thereby enabled Peter to heal the lame man (3:13). Peter exhorts the people to repent and turn to God so that they too might have "times of refreshment from the face of the Lord" (3:20). These times of refreshment almost certainly refer to the enthroned Messiah's ability to grant blessings upon his people through the work of the Spirit.

(d) The Repentant People of God in Jerusalem

Acts has significant episodes that narrate Jewish unbelief in Jesus as the Messiah of Israel (e.g., 13:46; 18:6; 28:28). However, readers of Acts should not ignore the presence of a large group of believers in Jesus located in Jerusalem. The Jews have not, then, entirely rejected Jesus. In fact, Luke narrates mass conversions of Jews throughout Acts, especially in the early chapters. In response to Peter's Pentecost sermon, Luke says that three thousand people were baptized and joined the church (2:41). Despite the Sanhedrin's attempt to eradicate the movement, five thousand come to faith in response to the disciples' preaching Jesus's resurrection from the dead (4:2–4). One of Luke's consistent summary statements throughout his narration of the disciples' proclamation of Jesus in Jerusalem is "believers were added to the Lord in increasing numbers—crowds of both men and women" (5:14; cf. 2:41) and "the disciples were, in those days, multiplying in number" (6:1, 7; cf. 12:24). These statements show that God's favor rests upon the church, and yet they also indicate that God's purposes for Israel have not been made null and void. When we encounter James's statement toward the end of the book, namely, that there are myriads and tens of thousands of Jews who believe in Jesus, we should not be surprised (21:20).[23]

Furthermore, Luke describes this repentant people as embodying the characteristics God had expected for his restored people. Take a look, for example, at Acts 2:37–47. At the end of Peter's Pentecost speech he claimed that God has established Jesus of Nazareth over the entire house of Israel as "Christ and Lord, this Jesus *whom you crucified*" (2:36). It should not escape the reader's notice that Peter reminds them of their culpability in rejecting the Messiah; thus, there is something of a second chance for repentance for Israel mediated through the proclamation of the apostles.[24] The peoples' question, "What then shall we do?" (v. 37b), is exactly the right response and is reminiscent of the questions asked of John the Baptist when he sought to prepare a repentant people in anticipation of God's coming in the person of Jesus (Luke 3:10–14; cf. 1:16–17, 76; 3:4–6). Just as John demanded a just and generous use of possessions as the right response of repentance, so here the repentant community will use their resources, food, and money in service of one another (2:44–45). Peter's response to the question, however, is that they should be baptized in the name of Jesus Christ. This is the first instance of what

23. This theme of the mass conversions of Jews to belief in Jesus is a foundational insight in the writings of Jacob Jervell.

24. Johnson, *Acts of the Apostles*, 60.

is a stable but flexible pattern throughout Acts, namely, a response of faith and/or repentance toward Jesus Christ that then results in the divine bestowal of the gifts of release from sins, the reception of the Holy Spirit, and salvation (2:38, 40, 41; cf. 8:36–38; 9:17–19).

In 2:41–47 Luke presents a summary scene of the early Christian community to show how the outpouring of the Spirit from the exalted Davidic king results in a people who fulfill the Lord's expectations for his people. That the early Christian community is a prophetic people can be seen by the manner in which its character traits resonate with the teachings of Israel's prophets. Thus, the gift of the Spirit that was anticipated by Israel's prophets produces a restored prophetic people of God. Those who have responded to Peter's proclamation of the Messiah are characterized as: a) repentant and having turned to the Lord (2:38; cf. Ezek 18:31; Joel 2:12–13; Isa 43:24–25); b) selling their possessions in order to provide food for one another (2:44–45; cf. Isa 58:6–7; Jer 5:28–29; 7:5–7; Mic 6:7–8); c) experiencing the presence of the divine through signs and wonders (2:43; cf. Joel 2:28–32; Deut 34:9–11; 18:15–18); and d) marked by unity, peace, and fellowship (2:42, 44, 46–47). In fact, Luke's use of this "unity language" to describe the Christian community suggests that this new group of peoples considers itself to be a fictive (i.e., non-biological) family who circulates its resources with generosity for one another.

If one reads Acts with Luke's Gospel also in mind, then one cannot help but notice that this group has implemented Jesus's actions and teachings on food, possessions, and hospitality. This can be seen in the church's "breaking of bread" (2:42), "selling their property and possessions and distributing them to anyone who had a need" (2:45), and "breaking bread from house to house and receiving food with joy and sincerity of heart" (2:46). Jesus was remembered as one who shared his saving presence with others through his meal practices, and his meals were occasions for inclusivity, the satisfaction of hunger, and joy (e.g., Luke 5:27–32; 7:36–50; 9:11–17; 15:1–2; 19:1–10; 24:30–35).[25] And Jesus had promised the twelve disciples that they would rule over God's people in God's kingdom precisely through "eating and drinking at *my table* in my kingdom" (Luke 22:29–30).[26] We are led, then, to see this description of the church in Acts 2:42–47 as the successful implementation of Jesus's teaching and ministry now continuing in the life of the early church.

This is the initial fulfillment of what Jesus had promised in Acts 1:8—"you will be my witnesses in *Jerusalem*." And while conflict and suffering at the hands of Israel's official leaders are impending, we are seeing here the restoration of Israel and the realization of God's kingdom precisely within Judaism. God has fulfilled his prophetic promises to send for the Spirit of prophecy, he has resurrected and enthroned his Davidic king to rule over Israel forever, and he has now brought about a prophetic community *within Jerusalem* that fulfills God's expectations for his people. Thus, despite the conflict and opposition that will characterize the relationship between Israel's so-called official leaders and the apostles, there is a restored people of God within Jerusalem.[27]

---

25. See further, Jipp, *Divine Visitations*, 223–35.
26. Jervell, "Twelve on Israel's Thrones," 75–112.
27. Jervell, "Divided People of God," 44–49.

REFLECTIONS

1. How does Acts continue the story begun in the Gospel of Luke?

2. Why is Israel so central to Acts?

3. What is the meaning and significance of God's resurrection of Jesus from the dead?

4

THE MESSIAH AND THE PEOPLE OF GOD

WE HAVE SEEN THAT the God of Acts is the God who elected Israel as his covenant people. God has now acted to fulfill the promises he made to his people. God has sent the Davidic Messiah and has raised him from the dead to rule over his people; God has poured out the prophetic Spirit upon those who believe; and God has reconstituted the twelve tribes by raising up twelve leaders to rule over his repentant people. God's people are defined as those who submit to the authority of the resurrected Messiah and his Spirit-empowered witnesses. Luke has already made a strong claim for the authority of the apostles by narrating their reconstitution and claim to represent Israel in Acts 1:15–26. They are the ones Jesus promised would "sit on thrones judging the twelve tribes of Israel" (Luke 22:30b). The rest of the narrative will portray them as acting with the power of the Spirit as articulated from the Joel quotation, which is programmatic for the identity and activity of the apostles (and other witnesses). In other words, the Spirit-empowerment of the apostles and witnesses is demonstrated throughout the rest of the narrative in that they prophesy, see dreams and visions, perform signs and wonders, and proclaim salvation to all those who call upon the Lord.

But tragically Acts narrates further conflict and division *within Israel*. There are mass conversions of Jews in Jerusalem, but there is also opposition to the gospel, which then immediately turns into violent persecution of the apostles. "Israel is becoming a divided people over the issue of the Messiah. This is the crisis."[1]

(1) PETER'S WARNING TO ISRAEL'S LEADERS AND THE PEOPLE (3:11–26)

Peter's speech, in response to those who are astonished at the healing of the lame man, describes how Israel's leaders acted foolishly and wickedly when they crucified Jesus who had done no wrong (3:13–14). Peter's charge that the people went along with their leaders and killed the innocent one, the very "author of life" (3:15), and asked for the release of a murderer is a powerful rebuke intended to elicit their repentance (3:19). Remarkably, Peter declares that despite their culpability, "you, along with your leaders, acted *in ignorance*" (3:17). The fact that the people acted ignorantly, however, slightly lessens the culpability of the people, but only for the purpose of offering them a second opportunity for repentance (see 3:19). Furthermore, their putting Jesus to death has, unwittingly, been the providential manner by which God has "so fulfilled all the things God had predicted through the mouth of all the prophets, namely, that the Messiah must suffer" (3:18). Peter's plea is that the ignorance of the people be replaced with the Spirit-inspired apostolic interpretation of God's plan as prophetically set forth in Israel's Scriptures (3:18, 24).

Peter declares that since God has fulfilled the promises of the prophets and since the people rejected Jesus out of ignorance, *now* is the time for the people to respond and

1. Jervell, *Theology of the Acts*, 36.

repent so that they may experience the covenantal and messianic blessings and not be removed from God's people. The imperatives in verse 19 contain the rhetorical function of Peter's speech: "therefore repent and turn" is a call to the people to recognize that they have rejected the Messiah and a warning to not make the same mistake now by failing to recognize the powerful work of the resurrected Messiah in the acts and teachings of the apostles. Peter declares that their experience of the promised blessings of the messianic age is contingent upon their repentance and embrace of Jesus as Israel's Messiah. Their repentance will elicit "the wiping away of your sins" (3:19b) and their experience of "seasons of refreshment from the presence of the Lord" (3:20a). The plural "seasons" most likely indicates that these are ongoing experiences of the Spirit's eschatological blessings upon God's people.[2] We have already learned that the pouring out of the Spirit is contingent upon the resurrection and heavenly enthronement of Israel's Messiah (e.g., Acts 2:33–36), so it is no surprise that these seasons of refreshment come from "the face of the Lord" (3:20b) and that "it is necessary for him [i.e., "Jesus the Messiah," 3:20c] to be received *in heaven until the times of the restoration*" (3:21a). In other words, the Messiah's heavenly reign is the cause of the messianic blessings upon God's people. The transformed community that has repented (2:42–47) as well as the healing of the lame man (3:1–10; cf. Isa 35:8–9) are the two examples Luke gives as tangible expressions of these times of refreshment. But Peter also indicates that these messianic blessings are a foretaste of the eschatological consummation when God will "send Messiah Jesus, the one designated for you" (3:20b). Jesus remains in heaven "until all the times of the restoration which God has spoken through the mouth of his holy prophets from long

2. See Sleeman, *Geography and the Ascension*, 108.

ago" (3:21b). The prepositional phrase should probably be translated "*until* the times of restoration" (3:21), as Peter's language here seems to point toward the eschatological return of the Messiah (cf. 3:20b). Peter's wording of Israel's future hope establishes a connection with the disciples' earlier questioning of Jesus as to whether it was at "this time that you will restore the kingdom to Israel" (1:6b).[3] Israel's restoration, then, is in process as the people experience the blessings of their enthroned-in-heaven Davidic king even as they wait for the consummation when he returns from heaven (1:10–11). While the details of 3:19–21 may be difficult, Peter's main point is not: God is fulfilling his messianic and eschatological blessings for his people *now*; therefore, the people must repent and turn to God so that they do not miss out on what God is doing.

If 3:19–21 focus on the messianic blessings that are contingent upon the peoples' repentance, vv. 22–26 have a strong note of warning or threat should the people fail to respond. Peter crafts a mixed citation, Deut 18:15, 18, and Lev 23:29, from the writings of Moses, one of Israel's prophets (cf. 3:18, 21b, 24), in order to establish that God has "raised up" (3:22) this prophet-like-Moses. Readers of Luke's Gospel remember that at the Transfiguration God's voice came from heaven to call the disciples to "listen to him" (9:35b), just as now Peter uses Deut 18 to call the people to "listen to him in everything he shall speak to you" (3:22b).[4] If they refuse to "listen to the prophet," Lev 23:29 declares that they "will be destroyed from the people" (3:23). Again, Peter reminds and warns them that all of their prophets have anticipated "these days" (3:24). Their continuance in the people of God will depend upon whether they listen to

3. Tannehill, *Narrative Unity*, 55.

4. Johnson, *Acts of the Apostles*, 74.

and obey the prophet-like-Moses who now works through the acts and teachings of the apostles.[5]

Israel's Scriptures testify that when God acts to bless his people Israel, this will be the means he uses to extend his blessings to the rest of the nations and families of the earth. This promise is, of course, set forth clearly in God's establishment of his covenant with Abraham in Genesis. While Peter's quotation of Gen 22:18 ("in your seed all of the families of the earth will be blessed") anticipates the extension of the messianic blessings to the Gentiles also, Peter's speech remains directly focused upon the covenantal blessings *for Israel*. Note the Israel-centric language in vv. 25–26: a) Peter's appeal to them that "you are the children of the prophets and the covenant" pleads with them to embrace the apostolic interpretation of their own Scriptures and covenants (cf. 3:18, 21b, 22–24); b) the God that Peter proclaims is the God of Israel, that is, "the God *of our fathers*" (3:25b; cf. 3:13a); and c) the Abrahamic covenant will soon be fulfilled as Gentiles will be received into God's people, but God has raised and sent his messianic servant to Israel *first* and in order "to bless you" (3:26; cf. Isa 49:5–6). But it is Jesus and only Jesus, God's servant, who "blesses" the Jewish people and thereby activates the blessings of the Abrahamic covenant.[6]

(2) THE DISCIPLES VS. THE JERUSALEM-TEMPLE LEADERS (4:1—5:42)

Who has the authority to lead and rule over the people of Israel? The disciples believe that God's resurrection of the

5. On the depiction of Jesus as a prophet-like-Moses, I have learned much from Minear, *Heal and to Reveal*; Moessner, *Luke the Historian*, 205–37.

6. Wendel, *Scriptural Interpretation*, 222–24.

Davidic Messiah and outpouring of the Spirit demonstrate that they are the leaders of God's people, whereas the Jerusalem authorities believe that the disciples have no such grounds for challenging the authority that has been mediated to them through their charge of the temple. Luke narrates the conflict between these two groups as something of a turf-war between two groups vying for the legitimate authority to teach the people of Israel.

At root, the conflict is primarily about the resurrection of Messiah Jesus and his ongoing powerful work through the disciples. Thus, the "priests, the captain of the temple police, and the Sadducees" are annoyed with the disciples "because they were proclaiming the resurrection of the dead in Jesus" (4:2). When the entire group of Jerusalem-temple authorities gather to question Peter and John, they ask, "By what power and by what name have you done this?" (4:7b). Readers familiar with Luke's Gospel may remember that the same leaders asked the same question of Jesus after his controversial act in the temple (Luke 20:2). Luke presents Peter's response with the following mini-speech (4:8–12):

> Then Peter was filled with the Holy Spirit and said to them, "Rulers of the people and elders: If we are being examined today for a good deed done to a weak man, by which means he was healed, let it be known to all of you and to all the people of Israel, that by the name of Jesus Christ of Nazareth, whom you crucified and whom God raised form the dead, by him this man is standing well before you. This one is the stone rejected by you the builders, he has become he cornerstone. And there is salvation in no one else, for there is no other name under heaven given to people by which we must be saved."

Peter's leadership presents a challenge to the temple authorities on at least three levels. First, the Holy Spirit continues to empower the disciples with the ability to give testimony to Jesus, and this results in a boldness of speech the authorities are helpless to stand against (4:7, 13). The threats and accusations made against the disciples are no match for the Spirit that continues to grant the disciples boldness of speech even amidst persecution (4:29–31). Twice Luke portrays Peter as responding to the threats with statements that they will listen and obey God only, even if it brings them into conflict with other humans (4:19; 5:29). If the disciples are characterized by boldness of speech, obedience to God alone, and the performance of powerful signs and wonders the Sanhedrin, priests, and Sadducees are characterized as motivated by jealousy (5:17) and fear of bloodguilt (5:28).

Second, the authorities cannot control or stand against the continuing activity of the resurrected and enthroned Messiah. The temple authorities look weak and pathetic as they try to silence the work of the Messiah who has healed the lame man. In response to Peter's speech Luke says "they had nothing to say in opposition" precisely because they themselves were able to see the lame man who was healed (4:14). They confer among themselves: "What would we do with these men? For an obvious sign has been done through them, clear to everyone living in Jerusalem, and we cannot deny it?" (4:16). They simply resort to ineffective threats and orders to stop teaching and talking about Jesus (4:17–18). The resurrected Messiah alone has the power to make humans well (4:11; cf. 5:15–16), to grant salvation and forgiveness of sins to humans (4:12; 5:31), to perform signs and wonders through the hands of the apostles (5:13), to create a repentant covenant people (5:31), and even—through his angel—unlock prison doors so that his witnesses can continue to "tell the people all about this life" (5:20).

Third, Peter's proclamation challenges the temple authorities to recognize their ignorance in crucifying Jesus of Nazareth lest they be found to be judged by God. Peter's quotation of Ps 118:22 ("this stone rejected by you the builders has become the chief cornerstone") demands that the temple leaders recognize that they are "the builders" who stand in the way of God's new work. At the heart of Acts 4 and Ps 118 is the theme of reversal: *You rejected* the stone, *but God* has made it the chief cornerstone. You murdered the author of life, but God raised him up (5:29–30). Jesus too had quoted Ps 118:22 to the temple authorities but he added the interpretive note, "Everyone who falls on that stone will be broken to pieces, but on whomever it falls, it will shatter him" (Luke 20:18). The chief priests and scribes got the point—they realized Jesus had spoken against them and began to plot for a way to kill Jesus (Luke 20:19).

Tragically for Luke's story, Israel's leaders remain unrepentant and recalcitrant in their opposition to God's restoration of Israel and his resurrection of the Messiah. They are playing the role of the enemies of the Messiah as they take their stand "against the Lord and against his Messiah" (4:26b; cf. Ps 2:1–3). Thus, they are in danger of being cut off from God's people for their opposition to the Messiah and his witnesses (3:22–23). Therefore, there is a crisis of division within Israel. Israel's temple leaders and many of the people have murdered the Messiah and continue to reject the offer of salvation through his witnesses (2:23; 3:15; 4:10; 5:30). But, as we saw in the last chapter, many Jerusalem Jews *have responded and believed in the Messiah* (2:41, 47; 4:4; etc.).

(3) STEPHEN'S ACCUSATION AND MARTYRDOM (6:8—7:60)

(a) The Prophetic Characterization of Stephen

Let's look at one more episode that further clarifies the conflict within Israel that has arisen between Jesus's witnesses and the unbelieving Jews. We will look at Stephen and the Hellenists in a later chapter, but here we should note that though he is not one of the Twelve, he is characterized as a faithful witness who carries on the ministry of Jesus. Stephen, as well as the other seven Hellenist leaders, are "full of the Spirit and of wisdom" (6:3) and are "men who are full of faith and the Holy Spirit" (6:5). Stephen is "full of grace and power" (6:8); Stephen's speech cannot be resisted due to his speaking "with wisdom and Spirit" (6:10). This should remind us of exactly how Peter and the Twelve have been characterized: Peter speaks and is "filled with the Holy Spirit" (4:8), and three times in chapter 4 Luke says they speak with boldness (4:13, 29, 31), so boldly that the Sanhedrin has no strength to oppose him (4:14). Stephen is said to be "performing great signs and wonders among the people" (6:8), and we have seen that the performance of "signs and wonders" is exactly what Joel prophesied would happen when the Spirit was poured out (Acts 2:19; cf. 2:43; 4:33; 5:12–15). But these "signs and wonders" are signs of the Spirit who is the powerful empowering presence of the exalted Christ with his people. The point here is that the description of Stephen (and the seven Hellenist leaders) demonstrates that, like the Twelve, they are carrying on the story of Jesus as his Spirit-empowered witnesses.

(b) Stephen's Trial

Now it must be emphasized—and we should not be surprised either!—that the leadership of Stephen is massively
successful: "The Word of God grew and the number of
disciples in Jerusalem increased greatly, and even a larger
number of priests became obedient to the faith" (6:7). Even
some of Israel's priests are responding to Jesus's witnesses!
But we are also not surprised that amidst the success there
is deep opposition to Stephen's ministry. Luke says that opposition arose against Stephen, and though they were unable to get the better of him in argument, they persuade
others to bring false charges against Stephen, namely, that
he is a renegade Jew. He speaks blasphemy against Moses,
God, the Law, and the Temple, they claim (6:8–15). We'll
look at Stephen's response to these accusations next, but the
trial ends in the stoning and death of Stephen. His accusers
are enraged at his speech, and when Stephen claims to see
God's glory and Jesus standing at the right hand of God,
they rush against him and stone him (7:54–60). Luke has
constructed this story of Stephen's trial and death in such a
way that it clearly recalls Jesus's own trial and death. Note
the following commonalities:

1) The characters involved: elders, scribes, and Sanhedrin
   (Acts 6:12; Mark 14:58)

2) False witnesses brought against Jesus and Stephen
   (Acts 6:13a; Mark 14:56–57)

3) Both falsely accused of wanting to destroy the temple
   (Acts 6:14; Mark 14:58)

4) Jesus says you will see the Son of Man . . . (Mark 14:62)
   and Stephen sees the Son of Man at the right hand of
   the Father (Acts 7:54)

5) Charge of blasphemy (Acts 6:11; Mark 14:64);

6) Jesus cries, "Father into your hands I commit my spirit" (Luke 23:46), and Stephen cries, "Lord Jesus, receive my spirit" Acts 7:59)

7) Both cry out with a loud voice (Acts 7:60; Mark 15:36)

8) Both intercede to God for their enemies' forgiveness (Acts 7:60; Luke 23:34)

The basic point of the similarities would seem to be that Stephen and the witnesses are *continuing the work of Jesus of Nazareth* in proclaiming God's word to his people Israel, and yet despite the second chance for repentance that God has offered to his people many within Israel are rejecting and opposing those who proclaim God's saving purposes.

(c) Stephen's Countercharges and Retelling of Israel's History

Stephen's speech made in response to the charges leveled at him elicit the hostility that results in his death. What did he say that so angered the Sanhedrin? I want to look at how Stephen's speech interprets the plot line of the OT, that is Israel's history, to demonstrate that he (and his fellow believers in Jesus) is not against Moses, Temple, and Law—but, rather his accusers, his enemies, are against Moses, Temple, and Law.[7]

First, Stephen interprets the history of Israel as one of rejection of God's prophet Moses, and this rejection of the prophet-like-Moses is occurring even now in their rejection of Stephen. Let's look at 7:17–43 to see how this works. Now, in order to understand Stephen's speech we need to recognize that his speech is operating typologically, or drawing patterns between Israel's rejection of the prophet Moses and the current rejection of Jesus (the prophet like Moses) and the apostles. In other words, Israel's history and

7. See here Sterling, "'Opening the Scriptures,'" 199–217.

specifically the story of Moses foreshadows and provides patterns for what is currently taking place in the narrative.[8]

Stephen reminds his fellow Israelites that Moses was growing in wisdom, and was powerful in word and deed (7:22), just like the Gospel of Luke tells us that Jesus was a prophet powerful in word and deed (Luke 24:19). Moses later visits his people trying to bring salvation to them, but they do not understand (7:23–26)—just like Jesus who visits his people for salvation but they do not understand. Stephen says in 7:26 that Moses tries to reconcile them in peace, and peace is one of the primary messages Jesus brings to the people in the Gospel of Luke (e.g., Luke 19:41–44). The people reject Moses, however, and declare that he is not their "ruler and judge" (twice, 7:27; 7:35) and "ruler and rescuer" (7:35). This language is very close to how Jesus is described in Acts: Peter refers to Jesus as "ruler and Savior" (5:31) and "holy and righteous one" (3:13–14). Moses is the one who performs "signs and wonders" and this is how Jesus is described in Acts ("Jesus of Nazareth, a man attested to you by God with deeds of power, wonders and signs that God did through him", 2:22; 10:36). The clearest point of comparison between Moses and Jesus is in 7:37 where Moses himself speaks of a prophet-like-Moses to come who will do the same things for Israel (quoting from Deut 18:15). And we have already seen Peter quote Deut 18:15 to describe God's acting of sending Jesus *the prophet-like-Moses* (Acts 3:22).

The point in the pattern is that as the audience's ancestors rejected the prophet Moses, the prophet who did signs and wonders among them, and who sought their salvation and liberation, so now the audience proves that they are indeed the "sons of their forefathers" in that they now are again rejecting the prophet-like-Moses, namely Jesus and

8. See here especially Johnson, *Acts of the Apostles*, 136–37.

his witnesses, who have come for Israel's salvation. Thus, Stephen is not against Moses; ironically, Stephen's opponents are the ones whose ancestors rejected Moses and now they are rejecting God's prophets once again. "You stiff-necked people with uncircumcised hearts and ears! You are always resisting the Holy Spirit just as your ancestors did, so you do also. They even murdered those who foretold the coming of the Righteous One; whose betrayers and murderers you have now become" (7:51–52). Thus, Stephen responds to the charge that he acts against Moses by declaring, "No! Moses himself testifies to a day when another prophet-like-Moses will be raised up. We have accepted this prophet and are his witnesses. You are the ones who go against Moses by rejecting this prophet-like-Moses" (my paraphrase).

Second, Stephen accuses his opponents of preferring idolatry instead of obedience to God's leaders. Stephen narrates that after their rejection of Moses, they constructed and offered sacrifices to the golden calves (7:40–41). As a result, God "handed them over to worship the stars of heaven" (7:42). Stephen draws upon Amos 5:25–27, which proclaims judgment upon God's people for worshipping the false gods of Moloch and Rephan (7:42–43). Ironically, he charges them with turning the Temple into an idol. Stephen declares that God's true dwelling place, the place where his glory resides, is in heaven where the exalted Messiah now dwells and rules. Again, Stephen criticizes not so much the temple itself as he does Israel's leaders' wrong evaluation and treatment of the temple as the sole dwelling place of God. In 7:48 he speaks of the Temple as something "made with human hands" (7:48), which is language the OT repeatedly uses to describe idols—and even in 7:42 we see that when Israel commits idolatry with the golden calf, the idol is referred to as "works of their hands" (7:41).[9] Again, Stephen

9. Pao, *Acts*, 207.

quotes Isa 66:1 to declare that God cannot be housed by something built by humans or by temples. Heaven is his true dwelling place.

Luke's narration of Stephen's death confirms the truthfulness of Stephen's radical claim about the glory of God being bound up not in one locale but with the exalted Jesus in heaven (7:55–60). Stephen looks "into heaven" (7:55)—we have seen this language repeatedly used to describe the locale of Jesus (1:9–11; 2:2, 5; 2:33), who is still present and active with his people from heaven. When he looks into heaven he sees "the glory of God," precisely that which the audience wanted to see as kept in the temple only. And the glory of God is associated with this Jesus in heaven at the right hand of God. And now it's for this that they finally stone him to death, for his claim that the glory of God is identified now with the exalted Messiah Jesus in heaven.

Our examination has demonstrated that there are a variety of ways of speaking about the relationship between Israel and the church that are lacking in nuance and fail to do justice to the story Acts tells. It is simply not true to say, "The church has replaced Israel as God's people," "Israel rejected Jesus and the gospel," or "the church is the new Israel." Luke's story demands that we do better in nuancing how we speak of the origins of the church. God has elected Israel as his covenant people and has made promises of peace, salvation, and restoration to them. Acts is concerned to show that God has indeed been faithful to these promises, primarily (not exclusively) through his resurrection/enthronement of the Davidic Messiah *and* his outpouring of the Holy Spirit. And numbers of Jerusalemites have indeed embraced the rule of this king, experienced the work of the prophetic Spirit, and are heirs of God's covenantal blessings. But, indeed, *not all Israel* has believed. The tragedy, for the story of Acts, is that many Israelites, especially their leaders, have rejected God's work and have thereby been cut off from God's people. Acts never allows us to stray too far from this theme, and as we turn to explore the narration of God's calling the Gentiles to himself, we will continue to explore how this theme relates to God's purposes for Israel.

REFLECTION

1. Would it be accurate to say that Acts supports the claim that "the church" is the "new/true Israel"?

2. Do you think Stephen is an apostate from Judaism? Are the charges made against him in any way legitimate?

5

SURPRISING EXPANSIONS IN THE PEOPLE OF GOD

THE READER OF THE Gospel of Luke knows that God's saving actions are for all people. God is the God who has elected Israel as his covenant people, but just as God promised Abraham, he will use Israel as a means of extending his salvation to the nations (Gen 12:1–4). The Gospel of Luke had made promises that hinted that the coming of Jesus would be "*a light of revelation for the Gentiles* and glory for your people Israel" (Luke 2:32). The angels who announced the good news to the shepherds declared that this Savior will bring "great joy that will be for all the people" (2:10). And whereas all the Gospel writers drew upon Isa 40:3 to describe John the Baptist's ministry of preparing a people ready for the coming of Jesus, only Luke quoted verse 5 of Isaiah, which promised that "all people will see God's salvation" (Luke 3:6).

But this mission to the nations is dependent upon God first restoring Israel. The resurrected Jesus had told his disciples that repentance and the forgiveness of sins will be proclaimed "to all the nations, beginning at Jerusalem. You are witnesses of these things. And behold, I am sending you what my Father promised. As for you, stay in the city until you have been empowered from on high" (Luke 24:47–49).

We have seen that Acts begins with a recapitulation of the risen Jesus's commission to his apostles, with the promise that they will be witnesses not only in Jerusalem but also in "Judea and Samaria" and "the ends of the earth" (Acts 1:8). The gift and empowerment of the Holy Spirit is the means whereby the witnesses will leave Jerusalem and cross all kinds of barriers and boundaries in their attempt to extend the good news of the Messiah to all people.

(1) THE SPIRIT AND CROSS-CULTURAL TESTIMONY

When the Spirit of God is poured out upon the believers at Pentecost, the Spirit is manifested in the miraculous ability to speak in unlearned languages.[1] The emphasis on language is obvious: tongues like a flame of fire rest on the believers (2:3); they speak in different languages/tongues "just as the Spirit *gave them the ability to proclaim*" (2:4); the Diaspora Jews are confused because they hear the believers speaking in their own dialects (2:8). The presence of the virtual table of nations (Acts 2:9–11a; cf. Gen 10; Isa 66:18–20) along with the note that the content of their proclamation is "the great deeds of God" (2:11b) indicates that the function of the Spirit is to empower the cross-cultural testimony of the witnesses.[2] The list of the Diaspora Jews "from every nation under heaven" is reminiscent of the Prophets' anticipation of a day when God would gather the scattered remnant exiled among the nations (see Isa 11:11–12; 43:5–6; 49:12; Zech 2:6).[3] Thus, Luke highlights the centrality of Jerusalem (cf. Acts 1:8) as

1. So Keener, *Acts*, 1.821.

2. On Acts 2:9–11 and the table of nations in Gen 10, see Scott, "Luke's Geographical Horizon," 483–544.

3. See Pao, *Acts*, 129–31.

Jewish representatives from the nations have returned to Jerusalem and there encounter the prophetic Spirit. If there is an allusion to the table of nations (Gen 10) and the story of God's confusing and scattering the languages at Babel (Gen 11), then here we should see that the multiplication of the languages serves God's purposes to reach all nations and languages.[4] Jerusalem is central not in the sense that Luke envisions the nations streaming to Jerusalem (Isa 2:1–4; Zech 8:20–23), but because Jerusalem stands as the geographical locale from which God will send the gospel to all nations. The Spirit's empowerment for cross-cultural proclamation is exactly as Jesus had foretold it in Acts 1:8— the Spirit grants the witnesses the power to proclaim the risen Messiah in new missionary settings. Thus, it is no surprise that the major role of Jesus's witnesses throughout the book of Acts is the powerful and prophetic proclamation of divine activity. We have seen in the previous two chapters that the Spirit empowers Peter and the apostles to give bold testimony to the gospel of the crucified and risen Messiah in Jerusalem (esp. 4:8–31).

(2) MOVING BEYOND JERUSALEM (ACTS 6–8)

Chapters 1–5 of Acts have narrated how the gospel took root, despite opposition, in Jerusalem through the testimony of the twelve apostles. We have seen now the fulfillment of the first part of Acts 1:8—"you will be my witnesses in Jerusalem."

- The twelve apostles have been restored and constituted as the leaders of the people.

---

4. Keener, *Acts*, 1.840–44.

- The promised Holy Spirit has been poured out in Jerusalem and Diaspora Jews from every nation under heaven have experienced the Spirit.

- The promise to King David, namely, that one of his descendants shall sit on his throne forever, has been fulfilled through the resurrection of Jesus and his exaltation to God's right hand.

- There is a repentant community in Jerusalem that implemented ethically what Jesus commanded and what the Prophets called Israel to do—unity, sharing of possessions, and repentance.

- The Lord has converted thousands of Jerusalem Jews to faith in Jesus Christ (2:41, 47; 4:4; 5:14)—mass conversions.

A transition occurs in Acts 6–8 where new Hellenistic Jewish leaders are given a share in this leadership. Stephen, Philip, and the other Hellenists are the pivotal and transitional Spirit-empowered witnesses who, just like the Twelve, continue the ministry of Jesus and take it beyond the boundaries of Jerusalem. We have seen that Stephen is characterized as a powerful prophetic figure who is filled with the Spirit and thereby performs signs and wonders (6:3, 5, 8, 10; 7:55). Luke shows that Stephen and the Seven are worthy as successors of the Twelve, and as continuing the ministry of Jesus, by placing them in charge over food and possessions. In other words, by them being placed in charge of "the daily food distribution" (6:2) or the "sacred daily meal," they are recognized and commissioned as having the same authority as do the Twelve (see Acts 2:42–47; 4:32–35).[5]

5. See also Johnson, *Acts of the Apostles*, 110–13.

(a) Stephen and the Scattering of the Church

Stephen and the others are obviously *Jews* but they are said to be *Hellenistic Jews*, almost certainly indicating that their primary language is Greek rather than Aramaic. Luke does not say anything that would suggest that the Hellenists had a different theology from the Twelve, but he does portray them as the ones who are uniquely situated to move the gospel into new territory. There is one component of Stephen's speech, in fact, which previews the Hellenists' conviction that God's presence is not bound to one particular geographical locale. Throughout his speech, Stephen argues that God's glory has never been bound to the land or the Temple. Israel's history demonstrates that God has always appeared to, and been with, his people outside the land of Israel. God's glory appears to Abraham in Mesopotamia (7:2); God was with Joseph in Egypt (7:9); Moses was "educated in all the wisdom of the Egyptians" and was forty years old when he visited his own people (7:22–23); God's angel appears to Moses in the burning bush at Mount Sinai and refers to the place as "holy ground" (7:30–33); God was present with his people during the wilderness in a moveable tent (7:44–45); and even Isa 66 declares that no human-made structure can contain God (7:48–50). Thus, even the history of Israel demonstrates that God is sovereign and free to extend his glorious presence to any geographical locale he sees fit. The theme comes to a climax, as we have seen, when Stephen looks into heaven and identifies the glory of God with the exalted-in-heaven Jesus who is enthroned at the right hand of God (7:55–56). Given that Jesus and the glory of God are spatially located in heaven and not restricted to one geographical locale, the way is now set for the glory of God to extend beyond Jerusalem. And it is the death of Stephen which results in a persecution of the church, and this persecution scatters the church (except the apostles) "throughout the land of Judea and Samaria" (8:1b).

(b) Philip, the Samaritans, and the Ethiopian Eunuch

The death of Stephen and the severe persecution of the church in Jerusalem leads to mission among those in Samaria (8:4). In fact, the frequent reference to Samaria indicates that Luke is intent on describing how the gospel goes to this specific geographical locale (8:1, 5, 14, 15, 25). This should remind most readers of the risen Jesus's promise: "You will be my witnesses in . . . Judea and Samaria" (Acts 1:8). Bible readers know that the relationship between Jews and Samaritans was difficult, to say the least. John's Gospel tells us, for example, that "Jews do not associate with Samaritans" (John 4:9) and even preserves a derogatory slur when it has Jesus's opponents say against Jesus, "Aren't we right in saying that you are a Samaritan and that you have a demon?" (John 8:48). The history of the Samaritans is complex, but it would seem to originate from when the northern tribes of Israel rebelled against Solomon and built Samaria as the capital and rival cult to the Jerusalem temple (1 Kgs 12:16–20; 16:24). When the northern tribes were carried into exile (2 Kgs 17:1–6), the Assyrian king brought foreigners into Samaria to intermarry with those from the northern tribes of Israel (2 Kgs 17:24). The Samaritans are perceived by Jews, then, as idolaters and unfaithful to the God of Israel. The Samaritans had their own temple (again, John 4:19–26), their own Samaritan Pentateuch, and their own claim to God's election of their people. Thus, the relationship was often one of avoidance and mutual hostility.

To return to Acts 8, we see that what happened in Jerusalem through the apostles happens now in Samaria through the Hellenist Philip. Philip proclaims to them "the Messiah," "the gospel," and "the kingdom of God and the name of Jesus Christ" (8:5, 12); he performs signs of healings and exorcisms (8:6–7, 13); he defeats the sorcerer Simon who had led the Samaritans astray through his hubris and black magic (8:9–11); and he baptizes those who believe (8:13). Much of the language here is stereotyped and compressed, but it is clear enough that Philip is now doing exactly what the Jerusalem apostles did in Acts 1–5.

Israel's Scriptures not only narrate the mutual hostility, they also look forward to the day when Judea and Samaria will be reconciled in peace and unity; they look forward to the day when Judea and Samaria will join together in worship of the God of Israel and obedience to the Davidic King (Ezek 37:15–28; Isa 11:12–13; Jer 31:17–20; Zech 8:13; 10:6–12). This is why the Jerusalem apostles, when they hear that Samaria received the word of God, send Peter and John to Samaria so they can pray and lay hands on them to receive the Spirit (8:14–17). This, of course, is not the usual way in which the Spirit is mediated, as the Spirit is usually granted when people believe and/or repent. Given the significance of the Samaritans being included in the people of God and joined together with the Jerusalem Jews of Judea, it makes sense that representatives of the Jerusalem church come to Samaria in order to confirm that the Samaritans are indeed united with them in the people of God! And perhaps they too need to learn and be reminded that the Spirit and the work of God is moving across borders and boundaries and into new territories that surprise even them.[6] The Samaritans are together now recipients of the promised Holy Spirit, united together as one people in peace, as they exist under the promised son of David who reigns on his

6. This point is not frequently emphasized, but see Skinner, *Intrusive God*, 56–57.

throne forever! Thus, when Luke refers to the entire region of Samaria receiving the word of God (8:14) and later provides a summary statement that "the church throughout Judea, Galilee, and Samaria had peace and was strengthened" (9:31), it seems likely that Luke intends to demonstrate that God's promises for the reunification of Judea and Samaria and their shared submission to one Davidic king has been fulfilled.[7] The story ends with Peter and John returning to Jerusalem, but on their way back proclaiming the gospel throughout the villages of the Samaritans (8:25).

The gospel has gone to Jerusalem (Acts 1–5), and now it has gone to the Samaritans (8:4–25). But the surprises continue as Philip now meets an Ethiopian eunuch. That this is a divinely ordained encounter is obvious from the fact that the story begins with God's initiative as he sends an angel to tell Philip to "go south to the road that goes down from Jerusalem to Gaza" (8:26), and it concludes with the "Spirit of the Lord snatching Philip away" (8:39). The point here is that God has ordained that Philip and this eunuch meet one another. We have already seen that Luke characterizes Stephen and Philip as prophetic witnesses who continue the ministry of Jesus, and the same holds true in this passage as Philip receives messages from the Spirit (8:26, 29), exposits Israel's Scriptures and proclaims the good news about Jesus (8:30–35), and baptizes the man (8:38). It seems to be of some importance to Luke that he emphasizes this characterization of Stephen and Philip since they are the ones God is using (not the Jerusalem apostles!) to spread the gospel beyond Jerusalem (cf. Acts 8:1–3).

But what about the Ethiopian's characterization? A few things stand out. First, while there are a variety of descriptors for ancient Ethiopians and many of them are

7. Especially helpful here are Pao, *Acts*, 127–29; Thompson, *Acts of the Risen Lord Jesus*, 112–16.

quite positive, one more frequently finds references to them as symbols of vice and sexual desire. Second, Luke repeatedly refers to the man as a "eunuch" (8:24, 34, 36, 38, 39). Eunuchs often served as royal officials, just as this man does, in part so that there would be no worries of sexual liaisons with the nobility. Despite this, eunuchs were frequently stereotyped as salacious and sexually ambiguous monstrosities. From the Jewish perspective, the Bible had spoken of eunuchs—those with "crushed testicles" or a "cut off penis"—as excluded from "the assembly of the Lord" and from worshipping God in the temple (see esp. Deut 23:1; Lev 21:16–23). Eunuchs were understood, then, to be excluded from the temple and even the worshipping assembly of the Lord! They were second-class citizens, not full participants in the people of God, unable to celebrate the festivals and make sacrifices in the temple. He is, then, a symbol of an outcast, one who conjures up exotic cultural and ethnic stereotypes.[8] But Israel's prophet Isaiah looked forward to the day when God would act on behalf of his people in a climactic way for their good, for their salvation. On this day, Isaiah declares:

> No foreigner who has joined himself to the Lord should say, "The Lord will exclude me from his people," and the eunuch should not say, "Look I am a dried-up tree." For the Lord says this: For the eunuchs who keep my Sabbaths, and choose what pleases me, and hold firmly to my covenant, I will give them, in my house and within my walls, a memorial and a name better than sons and daughters. I will give each of them an everlasting name that will never be cut off. As for the foreigners who join themselves to the

8. See here especially the illuminating and rich treatment of the man's gender ambiguity by Wilson, *Unmanly Men*, 113–49. See also, Pao, *Acts*, 140–42.

Lord, and to become his servants—all who keep
the Sabbath without desecrating it and who hold
firmly to my covenant—I will bring them to my
holy mountain and let them rejoice in my house
of prayer. Their burnt offerings and sacrifices
will be acceptable on my altar, for my house will
be called a house of prayer for all nations. (Isa
56:3–7)

When God acts for his people, then eunuchs, outcasts,
misfits, and foreigners will be included in God's people.
They "shall not be cut off" from my people! Note where the
Ethiopian man has just been—"he had come to Jerusalem
to worship" (8:27b). We don't know if he was able to worship or not, but assuming what the Bible says about men
with crushed testicles, he would not have been included
within the temple. But as we've seen, the glory of God cannot be housed in temples. As Stephen declared from Isaiah,
"Heaven is my throne" (Acts 7:49a), and Jesus who is identified as enthroned at the right hand of God in heaven *is
able* to manifest himself to the Eunuch. The Eunuch may be
rejected and excluded from worship in the Jerusalem Temple, but he's included in the people of God and converted
as a believer in Christ Jesus (8:38–39). Furthermore, Luke
does nothing to activate any negative cultural stereotypes
of the Eunuch. He is probably a Gentile who recognizes the
God of Israel as the one true God; he is reading the prophet
Isaiah; and he responds with enthusiasm to Philip's exposi-
tion of the gospel and seeks baptism for himself. In fact,
the Eunuch's question, "Look, there is water. What would
prevent me from being baptized?" (8:36b) draws attention
to the irony of resisting or fighting against God's purposes.
God just happened to ordain that Philip find this man, a
man who happens to be reading Isa 53:7–8, and God just

so arranged there to be a pool of water for baptism in a dry and desert place.

The Ethiopian Eunuch is one in a list of characters in Luke and Acts who may seem to have physical or ethnic "limitations" on membership in the people of God, but who encounter the saving presence of Jesus no matter: for example, the bent woman is a daughter of Abraham (Luke 13), Zacchaeus is a son of Abraham (Luke 19:1–10), the lame man for forty years (Acts 3:1–10), and now a man with crushed testicles (8:26–40).[9] No disability, no ethnicity, no geographical distance, nothing can exclude one from encountering the powerful presence of Christ who meets this man through Philip. Further, note that of all the verses from Isa 53 that Luke could have drawn our attention to he refers to the Suffering Servant who was despised, afflicted, rejected, and cast away. It may be that Luke draws a connection here between the experience of the suffering Messiah and the Eunuch who have both known the painful experience of exclusion.

The proclamation of the gospel has now expanded beyond the borders of Jerusalem through new witnesses, in surprising ways, and to unexpected peoples. God has used the Greek-speaking Hellenists Stephen and Philip to bring the gospel to Samaritans and outcasts. Luke's narration of the movement of the gospel into new territories "stokes confidence about venues the gospel has yet to find. Even the places that the book's original readers might consider new, unfamiliar, distant, or curious await the gospel."[10] We should not be surprised if God continues to use surprising people to bring the gospel to new places and widen the expansiveness of those included in the people of God.

9. Skinner, *Intrusive God*, 61.
10. Skinner, *Intrusive God*, 65.

(3) THE GOSPEL GOES TO THE GENTILES (ACTS 10:1—11:18)

By the time readers gets to Acts 10:1—11:18, they have been waiting patiently for the fulfillment of a promise that they have long anticipated. We saw that even in Luke's infancy narrative, Simeon had forecasted that Jesus would be a light for the nations. The Gospel concluded with Jesus's promise that repentance would be proclaimed "to all the nations" (Luke 24:47). In Acts 1:8 Jesus said that the apostles would be his witnesses to "the ends of the earth"—language that is used throughout Isaiah to refer to non-Jews (e.g., Isa 41:9; 45:22). At Pentecost Peter drew upon Joel 3 (LXX) to indicate that God's Spirit would be poured out on "all flesh" (2:17) and declared that God's promise was not only for those in Jerusalem but also for those who are far off (2:39). Peter also declared that God was in the process of fulfilling the Abrahamic covenant, promises which declared that "all the peoples of the earth" would be blessed by the seed of Abraham (3:25). God told Ananias that Saul was his chosen instrument that he would use to bring his name before "Gentiles, kings, and the sons of Israel" (9:15). There is, then, no surprise that Luke provides an account of how Gentiles are included within God's people.

Luke narrates the foundational event of the Gentiles' inclusion within God's people through a lengthy and alternating process of divine event and human interpretation. While the reader knows that God has willed the Gentiles' inclusion with the people of God, Luke is at pains to show *how* the church comes to discern and recognize this as God's will.[11] Luke narrates this event by showing how a

11. I reproduce here a brief portion of Jipp, "Beginnings of a Theology," 39–40. See further, Johnson, *Scripture and Discernment*, 89–108.

difficult and ambiguous event is rightly interpreted as divine activity by the characters in the narrative.

The story begins with two accounts of human experience of divine activity: Cornelius's vision of "God's angel" who commands him to call for Peter (10:3–6), and Peter's simultaneous vision while he is praying (10:9). In Peter's vision, he is commanded to eat clean *and* unclean food. In response to Peter's refusal, the voice speaks a second time: "that which God has cleansed, you shall not [consider] common" (10:15b). *God* is the one who has rendered insignificant the social divisions between Jew and Gentile, and his command requires that Peter's understanding of God undergo transformation. Luke again portrays the nonobvious nature of divine activity by emphasizing Peter's confusion over the vision.[12] Thus, as Cornelius's men arrive at Simon's home: "Peter was greatly perplexed over the vision that he had seen" (10:17; cf. 10:19). The repetition of Peter's perplexity over the meaning of the vision invites the audience to participate in construing its meaning. Though he does not yet understand its meaning, Peter obeys the voice: "now get up, go down, and go with the men with no discrimination, for I have sent them" (10:20). Peter's guests declare they have come as a result of a divine revelation to Cornelius (10:22), and that they have been "sent to bring you into his house and to listen to your words" (10:22b). Peter, still not yet understanding the meaning of the event, responds with initial obedience in that he invites Gentiles in to receive hospitality (10:23a).

The rest of the story narrates Peter's progressive growth in his ability to interpret God's activity within these events. So, finally within Cornelius's home, Peter declares that though it is not permissible for a Jew to associate with a Gentile, "*God* has shown me that I should not call any

---

12. See Gaventa, *From Darkness to Light*, 109.

person defiled and unclean" (10:28b). Through the shared visions and the shared hospitality with one another, Peter goes further in his declaration of divine identity: "Truly I now perceive that God shows no partiality" (10:34). Peter's statement can be understood as an insight into Israel's Scriptures (e.g., Lev 19:15–19; Deut 10:17–19) where God is described as impartial. But never had this axiom been used as the basis to provide for full inclusion of the non-Jew *qua* non-Jew within the people of God. Further, when the Gentiles experience the same outpouring of the Spirit that inspires ecstatic declaration of God's deeds (10:44–46), Peter rightly baptizes them since they have experienced the Spirit of God "just as even we had" (10:47). If the Spirit is the defining mark of God's activity and God's people, then who can stand in God's way if he has shared his Spirit with the Gentiles? The Gentiles have become participants in the exact same messianic gifts of the forgiveness of sins (10:43), the Holy Spirit (10:44–45), the ability to proclaim God's mighty deeds (10:46), and baptism (10:47–48).

Note that the narrator has not entered into the story to say, "God did" and "God said" but, rather, has allowed Peter to discern, interpret, and name God's activity in the surprising events.[13] Further, Peter's affirmation of God's activity has been the result of a process of *experience and encounter* of divine work: visions from heaven, hospitality with strangers, and the work of the Spirit. Though the event is surprising to Peter, Luke presents the inclusion of the Gentiles as aligning with the testimony of Israel's Scriptures (Acts 15:14–18), Jesus's own inclusion of outcasts within God's people (e.g., Luke 5:27–32; 7:36–50), Jesus's commission to preach "to all the nations" (Luke 24:47), and the initiative of the Holy Spirit (10:44–46; 11:15–17; 15:11).

13. Marguerat, *First Christian Historian*, 102.

Luke's narration of God's inclusion of the Gentiles marks a new point in the narrative of Acts. If Greek-speaking Jews, Samaritans, Ethiopian Eunuchs, and now Gentiles are part of God's people then there are no limitations in terms of peoples or geographical locales to which God's gospel can move. Perhaps some of the most important words of Acts are Peter's—"Jesus is Lord of all" (10:36).

(4) MISSION TO THE GENTILES (11:19–26 AND 15:1–21)

The Jerusalem believers confirm what *God has done* to bring the Gentiles into the people of God. This ratification is the foundation for the missionary journeys to the Gentiles. Acts 11:1–18 repeats a *second time* in summarizing form what the reader already knows from Acts 10. In his report to the Jerusalem church, Peter has no doubt that God has acted in these events: "God had given to them the same gift just as he gave us" (11:17). The story ends with the church responding by "giving glory to God, saying 'indeed, then, God has granted to the Gentiles repentance unto life'" (11:18).

The reader is not surprised, then, to find missionary activity to the Gentiles narrated in the very next episode in Acts. In Acts 11:19 Luke reminds the reader of how Stephen's death scattered the believers "as far as Phoenicia, Cyprus, and Antioch, speaking the word to no one except Jews" (11:19). But some of them begin to proclaim the good news about the Lord Jesus to the Greeks (11:20). In other words, when Stephen was martyred, this functioned as the impetus for the church and the Hellenists to speak about Jesus to other Diaspora Jews. But 11:20 says that some of them even began to proclaim "Jesus is Lord" to Greeks! If we didn't have the story of Cornelius, we might not be prepared for this to be acceptable; but at this point in the narrative we know that God has indeed included Gentiles. And now we see something new once again. This group of Christians in Antioch is composed of Jews *and* Greeks, and it mirrors the early Jerusalem community in some significant ways. Luke tells us that "the hand of the Lord was with them" (11:21), which is probably an allusion to the signs and wonders; a great many of them are believing and turning to the Lord (11:21b). Therefore, once again a Jerusalem representative comes, Barnabas, to confirm what has taken place. He "sees the grace/power of God" (11:23), he rejoices (11:23), he exhorts them to abide in the Lord (11:23), he finds Paul, and they stay in Antioch to teach and confirm this new Greek congregation in the faith. It is here that they are first called Christians (11:26).

The church in Antioch sends Barnabas and Paul on a missionary journey and they visit Cyprus (13:4–12), Pisidian Antioch (13:13–52), Iconium (14:1–7), Lystra and Derbe (14:8–20), and then make a return trip through these cities to strengthen the churches (14:21–28). Just when it seems as though the rest of the narrative will be devoted to Paul taking the gospel to new peoples and new places, a dispute arises from some Judeans who begin to preach the necessity of circumcision for Gentiles to be saved. Twice Luke repeats the content of their teaching: "It is necessary to circumcise them [i.e., the Gentiles] and to command them to keep the Law of Moses" (15:5; cf. 15:1). Luke uses the scene of a debate among the assembly to once again a) legitimate in a formal fashion the inclusion of the Gentiles *qua* Gentiles within the people of God; b) to establish the foundation for Gentile inclusion/cleansing within God's people as faith and the demonstration of inclusion is the same—outpouring of the Spirit (15:9–10); and c) to demonstrate the continuity that exists between Israel's Scriptures and the message of the gospel of the Gentiles.

Three characters have speaking parts in the debate. First, Peter once more in *summarizing* form declares that *God* chose him to declare the gospel to the Gentiles (15:7); God gave them the Holy Spirit, "just as he did to us" (15:8); and God has cleansed the Gentiles through faith (15:9). Once again, we see the theme of the futility of fighting against God appealed to when Peter warns them of the danger in testing God by imposing the Torah upon them (15:10–11). Second, Barnabas and Paul testify in the assembly. We are simply told that they narrate the powerful work that God had done through them in their missionary journey (15:12).

The high point is James's speech, which argues that there is a harmony between Israel's Scriptures and the mission to the Gentiles (15:13–21). James suggests that "the words of the prophets are in harmony" (15:15a) with how "God has intervened to take from the Gentiles a people for his name" (15:14). Luke has him appeal to just one prophetic text, namely, Amos 9:11–12: "After these things I will return and rebuild David's fallen tent. I will rebuild its ruins and set it up again, so the rest of humanity may seek the Lord—even all the Gentiles who are called by my name—declares the Lord who makes these things known from long ago" (15:16–18). How does this seemingly obscure prophetic text contribute to James's desire to affirm the Gentile mission apart from circumcision? The language of "rebuilding" and "restoring" anticipates a day when the Davidic kingdom and kingship would be restored. Unlike the time in exile where there was no Davidic king and no united people under the Davidic king's reign, the prophet Amos looks forward to a time when the people are united under the reign of a Davidic ruler.

Now it shouldn't be too difficult for us to put the pieces of the puzzle together. What Amos anticipated has been fulfilled in that a son of David has been placed on the throne, as the Messiah reigns from heaven over God's people. The Gospel of Luke begins with this as a promise to Mary: "he shall be great and called son of the Most High and the Lord God will give to him the throne of his father David and he will rule over the house of Jacob forever and his kingdom will have no end" (1:68–69). In Acts 2:30–31, Peter speaks of David: "Therefore being a prophet and knowing that God has sworn an oath to seat one of his offspring from his loins on his throne, he looked ahead and spoke of the resurrection of the Messiah that he shall not abandon him to Hades nor allow his flesh to see corruption" (cf. Acts 13:32–37). Thus, God established the Davidic kingdom. But it's the next part of the quotation that is critical for the direct argument. For Amos promises that once the promises made to David are fulfilled, then the rest of humanity will seek the Lord and "all the Gentiles" will call upon the name of the Lord (13:17). In other words, first restoration/salvation comes to Israel through Davidic king, *and then* promises go to the Gentiles.

Why, then, does James, after he insisted upon "not bothering the Gentiles from turning to God," go on to ask that a letter be written asking them "to abstain from pollution by idols, and fornication, and that which is strangled and from blood" (15:19–20)? One likely explanation is that he is not insisting upon keeping an abbreviated version of the Law as much as he is calling them to abstain from idolatry, and this would make sense as a particularly Jewish concern about Gentiles as idolaters and polytheists. This would clearly fit for the first call, to abstain from idols, but it also fits with "fornication" as this term can often be used to speak of sacred/cultic prostitution. The strangled animals and blood may also point to pagan cultic practices of the Gentiles. But it may also be insisted upon as a means of facilitating two distinct peoples living together.

REFLECTION

1. What stereotypes or stigmas might have been attached to the Ethiopian eunuch? To Samaritans? To the Roman centurion? What might be some contemporary examples of stigmatized people in our society?

2. Why was it such a surprising and momentous event when Peter and Cornelius shared hospitality with one another?

6

PAUL—MISSIONARY TO THE GENTILES

WHILE PETER DOMINATES THE first half of the book of Acts (chs. 1–12), it is Paul who is the main character for the latter half (chs. 13–28). Just as Luke made obvious the importance of the Peter-Cornelius episode by narrating it three times (10:1–48; 11:1–18; 15:7–10), so Luke narrates Saul's conversion on three occasions (chs. 9, 22, 26). While common Christian parlance speaks of the *conversion* of Saul, the literary dynamics of chapter 9 portray this less as a conversion and more as God's defeat of an enemy who has devoted his life to destroying the church. The risen Christ had commissioned his apostles to extend the gospel to the ends of the earth, but Saul's mission is exactly antithetical to what Jesus had proclaimed in Acts 1:8. Therefore, once again, Christ acts from heaven to advance the mission of the church. That this is a Christophany is clear from the fact that "light *from heaven*" flashes upon Saul (9:3; cf. 22:6–10) and the speaker identifies himself as Jesus and is referred to throughout as *Lord* (9:5, 10, 11, 13, 15, 17). Further, this is not so much a conversion as it is a call to mission on behalf of Christ. The risen Christ appears to Ananias, a disciple in Damascus who will care for Saul, and tells him, "This man is my chosen instrument *to take my name to Gentiles, kings, and Israelites.* I will show him how much he must suffer for my name" (9:15–16). Paul's transformation is evident immediately in that he right away begins proclaiming in the Jewish synagogues that Jesus is the Son of God and Messiah (9:20–22). The rest of Acts is primarily devoted to detailing how the risen Christ uses Saul to bear witness to Christ before all peoples. While Acts makes it clear that Saul will proclaim the gospel to Jews, it is his mission to the Gentiles that is emphasized. In the second retelling of his conversion, Luke adds the note that the risen Christ spoke to Paul: "Go, because I will send you far away to the Gentiles" (22:21; cf. 26:17–18).

Luke narrates three of Paul's extended missionary journeys. In Paul's first journey, he is accompanied by Barnabas (13:1–3) and travels from Antioch to Cyprus and then inland into Asia Minor (13:1—14:28); Paul then journeys back to Jerusalem for the conference in Acts 15. In his second journey he is accompanied by Silas and Timothy, and they make the bold move to take the gospel into Macedonia (15:36—18:22; the cities of Philippi, Thessalonica, Berea, Athens, Corinth); in the third journey, Luke primarily focuses upon Paul's missionary activity in Ephesus (18:24—19:41), though Luke notes numerous other stops in his travels. Rather than examine each of these journeys sequentially and in detail, let's look at four primary characteristics of Paul's missionary journeys.

(1) PAUL'S MISSION IS PROPELLED FORWARD BY GOD

We have seen repeatedly that the movement of the gospel to new places and new peoples is brought about through divine activity. We have seen this theme with Philip and the Samaritans (8:4–25), Philip and the Ethiopian Eunuch

(8:26–40), and Peter and Cornelius/the Gentiles (10:1–11:18). It is the Holy Spirit who speaks to the church in Antioch: "Set apart for me Barnabas and Saul for the work to which I have called them" (13:2), and this initiates Paul's first missionary journey. And again, it is God who directs Paul toward a geographical advance as he begins his second missionary journey while the gospel moves into Macedonia (16:6–10). Note the emphasis on divine initiative: "the Holy Spirit" forbids them to proclaim the word in Asia (16:6); "the spirit of Jesus" does not allow them to advance into Bithynia (16:7); they try to go to Mysia (16:8) when finally they have a vision of the Macedonian man asking for help (16:9–10a) and conclude that "God had called us to proclaim the good news to them" (16:10). Given that the church has navigated the ethnic limitations (Jerusalem council), Luke now shows us how the church transcends a geographical barrier by moving farther away from Jerusalem and going into the heart of the Greek world.[1]

(2) GENTILES DEMONSTRATE THEIR ACCEPTANCE OF THE GOSPEL THROUGH HOSPITALITY TO PAUL

We have seen in the last chapter that the Christian leaders have fully agreed that God has "made no distinction between us and them and has cleansed their hearts by faith" (15:9).[2] God has decided, then, to "take from the Gentiles a people for his name" (15:14). This *people* of God is now

1. On the way in which Luke is attentive to multiple ethnic differences as a means of advancing the gospel, see especially Barreto, *Ethnic Negotiations*.

2. What follows in this section is revised and abbreviated from Jipp, *Divine Visitations*, 240–47. I have benefited greatly here from Matson, *Household Conversion Narratives*.

inclusive of all Jews and Gentiles whose hearts have been cleansed by faith. In Paul's mission to the Gentiles the practice of hospitality functions as the positive Gentile response to Paul's message and highlights the social incorporation of the Gentiles into this new family.

(a) Lydia in Philippi (16:11–15, 40)

When Paul and his party arrive in Philippi they look for a prayer house (16:13). The "prayer house" is likely a reference to a Jewish synagogue. Luke never narrates whether they find a prayer house, though Paul does find a group of women and Lydia (16:13–14). Lydia's identity as a Gentile God-fearing *woman* will function as a test case for the Jerusalem council's affirmation of the gospel moving to Gentiles. Her response to Paul's proclamation is exemplary: Lydia "listened, [and] the Lord opened up her heart to pay attention to the words spoken by Paul" (16:14b). Lydia's response recalls Luke 24 where the disciples' "eyes are opened and they recognize [Jesus]" (Luke 24:31a) within the context of hospitality. Thus, as Jesus opened the disciples' eyes, so the Lord continues his revelatory activity with Lydia. The result is that "she and her household are baptized" (16:15a). Lydia's response to the Lord's opening her heart is to open her own doors: "if you have judged me faithful to the Lord, come in and remain in my house; and she compelled us" (16:15b). Lydia's hospitality is the right response to Paul's message as it is paired with her "faithfulness to the Lord," which recalls the agreement for the basis of Gentile membership in God's people at the Jerusalem council (hearts cleansed by faith, 15:9b). By "compelling" (16:15b) Paul to receive her hospitality, Lydia presses him to make good on his commitment to include Gentiles within God's people based on faith.

Paul's acceptance of Lydia's hospitality has significant social ramifications. Lydia's acceptance of baptism incorporates her and her household into the people of God. And likewise, the hospitality that occurs between these two distinct parties brings her household and the Christian movement into a binding relationship. Based on the dynamics of ritualized hospitality, one expects a new kinship group created out of former strangers that shares its resources. Lydia's demand (16:15) that Paul accept her hospitality is a request that Paul accept the integration of her household with the Christian messengers. That a kinship group has been created through hospitality is evident when, before Paul and Silas are forced to flee, "they entered into Lydia's house and saw *the brethren*, and encouraged them and departed" (16:40). Finally, Lydia's hospitality in her house creates a new space for the Christian religion other than the synagogue. The contrast between the house and the synagogue is evident in their attempt to proclaim in the latter but only establish the Christian cult in the former. The place where disciples and family are located who listen to the Word (16:14, 40), who share resources (16:15), and who function as a base for his mission has become the hospitable household (16:15, 40).

(b) The Jailer in Philippi (16:25–34)

The hospitality of a pagan household in response further establishes Christianity in Philippi in the conversion of the jailer in Acts 16:19–34. Following Paul's exorcism of a slave girl (16:16), Paul and Silas are imprisoned for "disturbing our city" (16:20) and teaching "customs which are impermissible for us" (16:21). The epiphanic cues of God's presence within the Philippian jail are obvious: Paul and Silas "praying and hymning to God" (16:25), "a sudden and great earthquake" that shakes the prison and "opens all the doors" (16:26a), the release of the prisoners (16:26), and the guard's response of trembling and falling down (16:29).[3] In this context, the jailer's response to them as "lords" and his question "what must I do to be saved?" (16:30) indicate that he sees them as connected to divine power. Given Luke's use of "Lord" to signify God and Jesus, and the pagan predilection to see deity manifested in powerful humans (e.g., Acts 14:8–18), the jailer's reference to Paul and Silas as "lords" indicates his confused but not entirely wrong conception of them as gods.

The narrative moves from the manifestation of the divine (16:25–29) to the jailer's acceptance of the Christian message in his home. Paul and Silas call on him to "believe in the Lord Jesus and you and your household will be saved" (16:31a), and they proclaim "the Word of the Lord with all in his house" (16:32). The Gentile house is the setting for proclamation (16:32) and the locale for hospitality (v. 34); it comprises the group of people who receive salvation, believe, and are baptized (vv. 31, 33, 34). The repeated mention of the house indicates that the establishment of Christianity in the house is the goal of the epiphany.

(c) Thessalonica (17:1–9)

The response to Paul's preaching in the synagogue in Thessalonica is mixed: some *Greek* God-fearers and women are persuaded (17:4), while "the Jews become jealous," set the city in an uproar, and form a mob to "attack the house of Jason" (17:5). Based on the mob's search for Paul and Silas at Jason's house and the reference to them as guests to "whom Jason has shown hospitality" (17:7a), it is evident that Paul and Silas have made Jason's house their base. In

---

3. Especially helpful on this episode of the prison escapes in Acts is Weaver, *Plots of Epiphany*.

other words, though we don't hear how this happened we see that a Gentile has once again welcomed and showed hospitality to Paul and Silas. Unable to find them at the house, "they drag Jason and some brothers" (17:6a) out of the house to the magistrates. The reference to "some brothers" inhabiting Jason's house again indicates that the house, not the synagogue, has become the locale for the reception of the Christian message and base of Paul's mission. The Jews bring charges to the magistrates against the Christians: "they are disrupting the world" (17:6b), they act against "Caesar's decrees" (17:7a), and they proclaim Jesus as a rival king (17:7b). The charges should be understood as the inhospitable rejection of the divine visit in Thessalonica. Luke has portrayed the antagonists of the Christian cult as rabidly inhospitable. They gather a crowd to purge them from their city (17:5), they attack the house of Jason (17:5b), they drag Jason and the "brothers and sisters" from the house (17:6a), and they seek to harm Jason's guests (17:7a). Thus, the divine visit and its messengers are rejected by the synagogue (17:2–3), but they are welcomed within the hospitable household.

(d) Corinth (18:1–11)

One finds similar dynamics in Paul's stay in Corinth (18:1–11). Paul first receives hospitality from the Jews Aquila and Priscilla (18:3) while he proclaims in the synagogue (18:4). When the Jews reject "the Word," Paul interprets their rejection as a sign of inhospitality and "he shakes out his garments against them" (18:6; cf. Luke 10:10–11), declaring, "From now on I am free to go to the Gentiles" (18:6b). The contrast between the synagogue as inhospitable to the Word and witnesses, and the "house" as hospitable and the locus of the Christian cult continues as Paul "transfers from [the synagogue] and enters into the house of a God-fearer named Titius Justus" (18:7a). The symbolic contrast between the inhospitable synagogue and hospitable household is suggested by the note that Titius's "house was next door to the synagogue" (18:7b). Heightening the contrast is that the establishment of Paul in Titius's house leads to the conversion of the synagogue leader and his household: "Crispus the chief synagogue leader with his entire household believed in the Lord" (18:8a). That they convert in the Gentile house and not the synagogue establishes the household as sacred space. Crispus and his household are representatives for "many other Corinthians who when they heard, they believed and were baptized" (18:8). Again, hospitality to the Christian messengers "becomes the concrete expression of household salvation." The establishment of the gospel in Corinth through hospitable households is confirmed by Paul's vision of the Lord (18:9), who declares "I am with you" and promises the cult's success in Corinth: "I have many people in this city" (18:10).

(3) PAUL'S GOSPEL PROVOKES CONFLICT

The risen Christ had indicated that Paul would suffer greatly for his name (9:15–16), and so it is no surprise that many Gentiles find his message to be profoundly disturbing as it challenges Gentile religiosity. Everywhere Paul goes, his gospel provokes conflict and disturbance among those who are committed to other deities.[4] Let's look at a few of these scenes in more detail.

(a) Paul and Barnabas in Lystra (14:8–20)

When Paul arrives in Lystra he does what Jesus and Peter did (Luke 5:17–26; Acts 3:10): he heals the lame man (14:8–10).

4. I have benefited greatly here from Rowe, *World Upside Down*.

In the ancient Mediterranean world—a world that was polytheistic and where the gods were often thought to be powerful and active in daily life—the intersection between the divine and the human was much more fluid than what we probably imagine. So it's not surprising that those with the most power were deemed divine, such as kings, heroic military generals, and healers. We've actually already seen an example of this, when Herod's proclamation is received as "the voice of a god, not a mortal!" (12:22). In antiquity, those who could perform miracles and wonders were often thought to be divine or agents of the divine. There are numerous stories in the ancient world of deities disguising themselves as humans, coming to test humans, and then either cursing them or rewarding them based on how the humans treated the disguised deities. Thus, the Lystrans claim, "The gods having become like men have come down to us," and their religious response to confess Paul and Barnabas as Zeus and Hermes and then make sacrifices to them is a powerful but unsurprising affirmation of their pagan, polytheistic religiosity. They think that the gods have disguised themselves and come to inspect their behavior, and so the appropriate response is to sacrifice/worship these disguised deities.

When Paul stops them from sacrificing and rends his garments, Paul himself engages in a powerful rejection of the pagan worldview and calls for a *total and complete reconfiguration of their theology*.[5] It will not be enough to engage in some tweaking of one's thoughts of the divine, to add or change a ritual, or to add a new piece of information, to recognize a new deity or two. Paul and Barnabas are calling for a complete transformation of how they understand God. When Paul calls their actions "futile/foolish"

5. Again, see the helpful analysis by Rowe, *World Upside Down*, 18–24.

he is aiming at the very foundations upon which Gentile religiosity is built.[6] That Paul is not calling them to religious reform is indicated by his call "to turn" or "to convert" to a new way of life. The basic and foundational problem of the pagans is that they do not have an ontological wedge or separation between God and humanity. They do not know the one God of Israel. Further, by calling them to turn to "the living God" (singular), Paul and Barnabas characterize the pagan gods as dead—they do not have the power to give life. To be "the living God" is to be Creator, to possess life-giving power to give rain, sustenance, and so-forth (14:15, 17). In the ancient world, Zeus was the giver of good things, of life, of rain, and sustenance. But Paul characterizes Zeus as dead—or at least not "the living God." Divine power belongs only to one deity—to the God of Israel who has demonstrated his power and salvation climactically through his Son and Lord, Jesus the Messiah. No other narrative, no other religious cult, no other competitor can stand. It is no great surprise, then, that the result of this call for total and complete theological reconfiguration is that Paul is stoned and dragged out of the city (14:18–19).

(b) Paul in Ephesus (19:1–41)

Paul's eighteen-month stay in Ephesus is described by Luke with a string of vignettes that all describe the powerful work of the risen Christ/the name of Jesus through the work of Paul. Thus, Paul takes a theologically deficient

---

6. "For you know that you were redeemed from your *empty way of life* inherited from the fathers, not with perishable things like silver and gold" (1 Pet 1:18). "They themselves report what kind of reception we had from you: how you turned to God from idols to serve the living and true God, and to wait for his son from heaven, who he raised from the dead—Jesus, who rescues us from the coming wrath" (1 Thess 1:9–10).

fringe group of John's disciples and baptizes them "in the name of the Lord Jesus" (19:5). Paul is the powerful person who performs signs and wonders and proclaims "the word of the Lord" in the lecture hall of Tyrannus for two full years (19:10). The handkerchiefs and aprons that have touched Paul are able to transmit healing power (19:11–12). He defeats the Jewish exorcists who want to invoke "the name of the Lord Jesus" (19:13) for their own ends, with the result that "the name of the Lord Jesus became praised" (19:17). The "name of the Lord Jesus" cannot be used as a formulaic magical incantation, but is only connected with authentic apostles, prophets, and witnesses. Authentic power, healing, and exorcism only belong to those who "proclaim the kingdom of God" (19:8). And after the magic books are burned, "the word of the Lord" grew strong and mighty (19:20). So, throughout the time in Ephesus, there are a string of interesting stories that all center upon how Paul, as the agent of the Lord Jesus, triumphs over any powers that stand against the gospel.

Luke offers one more reaction to the Way in Ephesus in 19:23–40. Once again, the reaction to Christianity is one of conflict: "there was no small disturbance concerning the Way" (19:23). This silversmith Demetrius, one whose very livelihood depends upon the market for idols—little statuettes of the goddess Artemis—is worried and rightly so. He claims that Paul's preaching has "misled a considerable number of people by saying that gods made by hand are not gods. Not only do we run the risk that our business may be discredited, but also that the temple of the great goddess Artemis may be despised and her magnificence come to the verge of ruin—the very one all of Asia and the world worship" (19:26b–27). In fact, Paul doesn't say anything that would surprise the reader of Acts. Does Paul persuade and seek to turn away all of Asia from serving idols? His encounters in Lystra (14:8–20), Philippi (16:16–18), and Athens (17:16–34) would suggest that he does. In fact, Demetrius's claim that Paul teaches that gods made with hands are not real gods is almost a direct quote from Paul's speech in Athens: "this Lord of heaven and earth does not dwell in handmade temples" (17:24), and God cannot be imaged through material resources (17:29). Is Demetrius right that the implications of Paul's teaching will be bad for his business?[7] Absolutely! Demetrius is absolutely right that the message of *one Lord Jesus* invested with full, supreme power, who dwells and resides not in temples but in heaven at God's right hand is a threat to their practice, business, and ultimately "the temple of the great goddess Artemis" (19:27). Note that the Christian message is not a spiritual timeless reality—accept Jesus into your heart and you will have a better life. It has real political and economic consequences. It involves ultimate allegiances that bring one into conflict with other aspects of society. It involves economic practices that are different from the world. Demetrius and the Ephesians recognize this, for in response to his speech Luke tells us "they were filled with rage and began to cry out, 'Great is Artemis of the Ephesians!'" (19:28). The city turns into a confusing mob scene as they chant to Artemis for two hours (19:32).

(c) "They Are Saying There Is Another King—Jesus" (17:7b)

The conflict continues throughout Paul's missionary endeavors. Throughout Acts there is a conflict between the apostles' healing powers and signs and wonders with the magic and sorcery performed by the opponents of the faith (e.g., 8:18–24; 13:4–12). We see the conflict again in Philippi where Paul exorcises a slave-girl who is being used

7. See Hurtado, *Destroyer of the Gods*, 24.

as a vehicle for mantic oracles. Note the contrast between her fortune-telling capabilities and the name of Jesus Christ (16:18). Thus, her masters accuse them of "troubling our city" (16:20) and "proclaiming customs which are not permissible for us to receive nor for a Roman to practice" (16:21) and so they are jailed. In Thessalonica, the house of Jason is attacked, resulting in chaos and the accusation that the apostles have "turned the world upside down" (17:5–8). In Ephesus, Paul's proclamation results in a mob uproar (19:21–41). Whatever the reason, the message of the gospel results in uproar, division, and schism in these cities. Why? What is it about the message of the gospel that is so problematic and disruptive to pagan culture?

A good place to start in answering this question is with Paul in Thessalonica. Note the charges that are brought against Paul and Silas after they have proclaimed that Jesus is the Messiah (17:2–3). An uproar divides the city once again, and it is claimed that "these men are turning upside down the *world* . . . and they all act against the decrees of Caesar saying Jesus to be another/different king" (17:7). If Jesus is *the* king, then, by implication, Caesar is not. And throughout the book of Acts we have seen that no one else but Jesus-Messiah-King-Lord has true claim to kingship/lordship. Herod (Acts 12), Simon Magus (Acts 8), Simon-bar-Jesus (Acts 13), and the mantic slave-girl with the Pythonian spirit (Acts 16) are all false pretenders. So the charges are not entirely wrong—if Jesus *is* King, then he is the singular ruler. And this confession is not surprising given what we've seen already in Acts. We've seen repeatedly that Jesus is *the* Davidic King who inaugurates God's kingdom. God promises Mary he will give Jesus the throne of David (Luke 1:32–33); he is confessed as king during the triumphal entry (Luke 19:28–40); he fulfills the promises made to David as he now reigns as king in heaven (Acts

2:30–36; 13:32–37); and hence the message of Jesus and the disciples is the kingdom of God (Acts 1:3; 8:12; 19:8, 25; 28:30–31). Jesus is King, and the reality that attends his life, death, and resurrection is named the Kingdom of God. Christian mission entails nothing else than the proclamation of this new King and Kingdom. Proclaiming this new king and entering into this kingdom are not simply "spiritual" as opposed to material realities. For the confession of this king who rules over this kingdom of God entails a complete reorientation of one's life. If Jesus is king, then Caesar, Herod, Zeus, Hermes, and miracle-workers like Simon Magus and Elymas are emphatically not! If Jesus is king, then true worship is not about sacrifices and temples (Jewish *or* pagan), but entails confessing him and worshipping him as Lord of all. If Jesus is king, then authentic worship consists in the practices he taught: sharing possessions, prayer, testimony, and hospitality. It is for this reason that the proclamation of him as King indeed results in remarkable conversions but it also produces massive rejection, division, and conflict with the culture and standards of the rest of the Empire.

(4) PAUL'S MISSIONARY PROCLAMATION WORKS WITHIN THE RELIGIOUS LOGIC OF THE GENTILES

While Paul's mission is successful in planting churches throughout the Gentile territories and lands, the emphasis of Acts is, as we have seen, primarily upon the way in which the proclamation of Jesus results in conflict and confusion. And yet Paul is also portrayed as working within the cultural and religious logic of the people he encounters. We have seen one example of this already, namely, the way in which hospitality to strangers—which was considered one of the premier virtues of Greeks and Romans—functions as an appropriate *Gentile response* to Paul and his message. Luke portrays the Maltese as appropriately responding to the incarcerated Paul with "philanthropy" by building him a fire in order to keep warm and then providing for his needs and assisting him on his way to Rome (28:1–2, 9–10). Paul's remarkable displays of power testify in ways that would make sense to pagans that the God of Israel and the Messiah are more powerful than competing sorcerers (13:4–12), mantic oracles (16:16–18), magic (19:18–20), and vipers (28:3–6).

But the scene where Paul is most clearly depicted as entering into the cultural and religious logic of his Gentile audience is his famous speech in Athens (17:16–34).[8] On the one hand, the introduction to Paul's speech prepares us for more conflict. Luke says Paul's spirit was "deeply provoked when he saw that the city was full of idols" (17:16). The philosophers accuse him of piecing together scraps and of being a philosophical dilettante (17:18). His audience clearly misunderstands his teaching about Jesus's resurrection from the dead, as they think he is trying to introduce foreign *deities* (plural)—"Jesus and Anastasis" (the Greek word for resurrection, 17:18b). The depiction of one who is debating with anyone who happened to be in the Athenian agora (17:17) and the charge that he is "introducing foreign deities" is eerily reminiscent of the Athenian philosopher Socrates, who was tried and put to death for similar charges. Likewise, within Paul's actual speech he possibly commends their *deep religiosity* or, more likely, charges them with *superstition*. The Greek word is ambiguous, but given that superstition was defined as excessive and ignorant worship, Paul's charge that the Athenians "worship in

8. My fuller interpretation of this text can be found in Jipp, "Paul's Areopagus Speech," 567–88.

100

ignorance" (17:23; cf. v. 29) suggests Paul is chiding them for wrong worship.

Paul's speech, however, works within some of the common assumptions of the philosophers, particularly the Stoics (17:18). Stoics would have been deeply sympathetic to a theology that emphasized: a) the singularity of God/monotheism (Acts 17:24); b) a philosophical critique of religion and the attendant uselessness of temples and sacrifices (17:24b–25); c) the unity of humanity (17:26a); d) providence and the determination of the historical seasons (17:26b); and e) humanity's union with God (17:28–29). Paul even appeals to Stoic poets and philosophers to make his point in 17:28: "For in him we live and move and have our being, as some of your own poets have said, 'For we are also his offspring.'" Paul here seems almost certainly to be citing the Stoic poet Aratus and possibly alluding to the Stoic Cleanthes's famous "Hymn to Zeus" in order to justify his claim that it is *humans* who image God's nature and not gold, silver, or stone images (17:29). *But* the Athenians have worshipped these images, and so Paul warns them that God is commanding them to turn from their false worship (17:30). The high point of Paul's speech centers, unsurprisingly, on God's resurrection of Christ from the dead: "God has set a day when he is going to judge the world in righteousness by the man he has appointed. He has provided proof of this to everyone by raising him from the dead" (17:31). It is here that Paul's speech is interrupted, and some mock him while others believe (17:32–34). It is Christ's resurrection and heavenly enthronement that places him in a position of universal power and authority and thereby is the act that demands that all turn to him (e.g., 2:22–36; 3:11–26; 5:27–32). Paul's speech works within the categories and logic of the Stoic philosophers, and yet as it does so it disrupts their beliefs and allegiances about ultimate authority and power.

(5) PAUL IS THE MODEL PASTOR
FOR HIS CHURCHES

The final characteristic of Paul's mission to the Gentiles that we will examine concerns Paul not only as a church planter but as a pastoral model for those who lead and serve within the local churches. Though less memorable and easier to lose sight of given the vivid depictions of Paul's initial planting of his churches, Luke describes Paul as continuing to teach, edify, and build up his churches. We know this to be the case from Paul's letters, which are basically attempts to socialize his churches into the ins and outs of the Christian gospel, but we see it in Acts as well. For example, after Paul's initial planting of the churches in Asia Minor (in his so-called first missionary journey, 13:1—14:20), he returns to his churches in order to "strengthen the disciples and encourage them to continue in the faith, telling them, 'It is necessary to go through many tribulations in order to enter into the kingdom of God'" (14:22b). Paul and Barnabas then appoint elders in all of the churches and commit them to the Lord through prayer and fasting (14:23). Luke portrays Paul again as taking the opportunity to teach and encourage his churches in Macedonia on his way to Greece (20:1–3). But the primary way in which Luke impresses the role of Paul as pastor upon his readers is through Paul's speech to the Ephesian elders delivered in Miletus (20:18–35).

But before we look at Paul's speech to the elders, I want to point out how Luke uses the seemingly bland travel statements of Paul to frame the speech for an important purpose. Note that before the speech (20:1–16) and after the speech (21:1–15) there are some long and fairly detailed descriptions of Paul's journeys. Luke could have narrated this with *much less detail* than he does, as we have seen him do on other occasions (e.g., Acts 16:11–13; 13:4, 13). So, what is the purpose of these travel descriptions? The point is fairly simple but nevertheless important: through Paul's travel reports Luke shows the success of the Pauline mission to the Gentiles by reporting numerous cities and regions that are now filled with Christ-followers who support Paul and who perform explicitly Christian activity. And these Gentile Christians do what the Jerusalem Christians did in Acts 2:42–47 and 4:32–35. So we see Gentiles who are devoted to the teaching of Paul the apostle (20:7–12): they are engaging in the breaking of bread (20:7, 20:11), they bestow hospitality upon Paul (Philip in 21:4, 7–8, 10), and they are devoted to prayer and prophecy (21:5, 9, 11–14). Through these details, which frame Paul's final speech to Christians, the reader is encouraged to see Christian communities filled throughout the Mediterranean world that do what the original apostles and church did in Jerusalem.

When Paul stops in Miletus, about fifty miles south of Ephesus, he invites the Ephesian elders to hear him speak what is his last speech to a church in the book of Acts. Paul's discourse functions as a representative speech to already established Christian leaders, and it takes the form of a farewell address/last testament (similar to what Jesus gives in Luke 22:14–38), as it provides: a) a short sketch of Paul's life and ministry (20:18–21); b) a prediction of his own destiny (20:22–23, 25); c) a foretelling of what will befall the church after his life (20:28–30); and d) exhortations on how to behave (20:28, 31) with Paul as the model for their behavior. We can understand Paul's speech by looking at three aspects of Paul's presentation of himself as a model pastor for the church to follow.

(a) Paul Presents Faithful Ministry as a Life of Service on Behalf of the Gospel

Paul's ministry is entirely that of a *witness* who does not exalt or preach himself, but only the gospel of Christ. Note the language in 20:35—"all these things I have left for you as an example." But this example is not one of self-exaltation, for he has been *the Lord's servant* in his ministry (20:19). He has modeled "humility" through serving his churches with labor of tears (20:19b) and he has not drawn back despite persecution from the Jews (20:19b). He has proclaimed the full intent of God and his purposes, both publicly and in houses (20:20). He proclaims repentance to God and faith in Jesus Christ (20:21). He bears witness to the gospel of the grace of God (20:24). The message has been that of the "kingdom of God" (20:25), that is to say, not a human message but a message of God's rule through the exalted Messiah. He proclaims "the whole purpose of God" (20:27). He has not coveted anyone's money (20:33), but has worked hard with his own hands to earn his keep (20:34). Ultimately, his life and ministry are grounded in the ministry of Jesus, made clear by the fact that he bases his behavior upon the very "words of the Lord Jesus" who said, "It is more blessed to *give* than *to receive*" (20:35b).

(b) Paul Presents Faithful Ministry as Involving Endurance Amidst Suffering

Paul's speech is given under the dark auspices of Paul journeying to Jerusalem. Again, we remember that Jesus journeyed to Jerusalem where he suffered and was crucified. Note 20:22–23: "and now I myself am bound by the spirit to go to Jerusalem not knowing the things which will happen to me, except that the Holy Spirit testifies to me in every city that bonds and tribulations await me." Note the reference to "every city" testifies to Paul of suffering—in other words, his entire missionary and pastoral ministry has been one of suffering (Acts 14:27!). Yet the life of a faithful missionary/pastor requires 20:24!—testifying to the gospel and grace of God, fidelity to the commission received from the Lord Jesus, considering one's life of no account. Truly, one is a slave of the Lord as one considers his ministry supreme above even one's own life and desires (20:19, 24).

(c) Paul Presents Faithful Ministry as Guarding the Church from Error and Apostasy

Paul knows that false teachers will invade the church, with even the possibility that some will be led astray later by some of the elders who are present in their midst (20:29–30). The charge to the elders, then, is incredibly important as they are to watch out and keep guard on behalf of "the church of God, which Jesus acquired with his own blood" (20:28). Again, Paul holds up his own example of having labored in the Ephesian church for three years, edifying and seeking to guard and strengthen the church (20:31). Ultimately, however, it is God who protects and builds the church that he has sanctified (20:32).

REFLECTION

1. What role did hospitality and the home play in Paul's missionary strategies?

2. Was the Christian movement political? Did it challenge culture and society in any meaningful way?

3. Did Paul engage in any positive relationships or friendships with non-Christian gentiles? If so, what does this contribute to our view of Paul and his ministry?

7

PAUL—MISSIONARY TO ISRAELITES AND KINGS

PAUL IS REMEMBERED AS the "apostle to the Gentiles"—and with good reason! But the reader of Acts quickly discovers that Paul spends just as much time and effort proclaiming the gospel to Israel. And we have seen that the risen Christ had foretold that Paul would testify to "kings and the sons of Israel" (9:15b). Paul's consistent practice, frequently frustrated though its attempts may have been, was to find a Jewish synagogue where he could testify to the resurrected Messiah.

(1) PAUL PROCLAIMS THE GOSPEL TO ISRAEL (13:13–41)

Luke provides the readers with a representative scene and sermon for how Paul proclaims the gospel to the sons of Israel in the synagogue at Acts 13:13–41. This is Paul's first speech, as well as the first speech recorded in the first missionary journey (13:1—14:28). Paul and Barnabas enter into the city of Pisidian Antioch, the province of Galatia's city known as "Little Rome," namely, the Roman colony of Pisidian-Antioch. But despite the city's historic relationship to Rome, Luke immediately moves his reader to the Jewish synagogue (13:14). Paul's speech takes place within the weekly Sabbath ritual of "reading of the law and the prophets" (13:15a). Paul's speech ensues when the synagogue leader asks Paul if he would deliver a "word of exhortation to the people" (v. 15b). Both the narrator's seemingly insignificant request that Paul speak "to the people" (13:15) as well as Paul's decision to refer to his audience as "Israelites" (13:16) and "brethren" (13:26, 38) functions to make the point that the historic Israel of God is embodied in Paul's contemporary audience.

Paul's sermon begins by presenting a mini-history of God's people, whereby Paul emphasizes God as beneficently electing and caring for his people Israel. Paul's election theology is explicit in his first sentence: "The God of this people Israel chose our fathers and exalted the people" (13:16). Throughout the sermon, God is the subject who cares for his people Israel: he compassionately leads his own people out of Egypt (13:17), provides for them in the wilderness (13:18), gives them land for an inheritance (13:19), and grants them judges and prophets (13:20). Second, without so much as even a mention of Torah, Sinai, or Temple, Paul orients God's climactic actions for Israel in relation to King David (13:21–22). God has "raised up David" as the king who will do that which God desires (v. 22b). As God elected Israel as his people, so God elected David as the monarch of his people. The pinnacle of the argument comes in v. 23 where Paul roots his message about Jesus in Israel's traditions about David: "From this person's seed, according to the promise, God has brought to Israel the Savior Jesus." This language of "promise" and "seed" alludes to the promises made to David in 2 Sam 7:12–14 where God declares that one of David's "seed" will have his kingdom established forever (7:12; cf. 2 Sam 22:51; 1 Chr 17:4–14; Ps 89:20–38).

This aspect of Paul's selective historical review will be of further importance when we examine 13:32–33.

The most striking component of the speech's first stage is that it situates Jesus within Israel's election history, not only as the promised heir of David's throne, but as the long-awaited *Savior* of Israel (13:23b). One might expect, based on the emphasis on the Davidic promises, that Paul would, instead, use a royal designation such as "Messiah" or "Son of God." "Savior" is a distinctively Lukan title for Jesus, and it comports well with Luke's overall concern to narrate how the message of Israel's Davidic King will be good news for the Gentiles. Thus, Paul's thesis is given in verse 26: "Men, brothers, sons of the family of Abraham, and those among you who fear God, the word of this salvation has been sent forth to us." While Luke concentrates upon the promises made to David, it is God's election of the people Israel, through the promises of descendants made to Abraham, which sets the wider context for God's salvation history. Paul recounts the basic Christian message concerning Jesus's death and resurrection, familiar to readers of Acts from earlier sermons (e.g., Peter in Acts 2:22–36) and to those familiar with the Synoptic Gospel's Passion Narrative (e.g., Luke 22–23).

The high point of the proclamation is the simple statement in 13:30: "But God raised him from the dead." What does this resurrection of the Messiah mean? Paul, like Peter in Acts 2:22–36, interprets God's resurrection of Jesus from the dead as God's fulfillment of the promises he made to David. So Paul explains (13:32–37):

> We also are proclaiming to you the good news of the promise made to the fathers, that God has fulfilled this for us, their children, by raising up Jesus. Just as even in the second Psalm it has been written, "You are my son. Today I have

begotten you." And because he raised him from the dead, no longer to return to corruption, so he has spoken, "I will give to you the holy and faithful things of David." And therefore, in another place he says, "You will not give your holy one to see corruption." For David, who served the will of God in his own generation, fell asleep and he was added to his fathers and he saw corruption. But the one whom God has raised, he has not seen corruption.

One might expect that the "promise made to the fathers" would be associated with the patriarchal promises made first to Abraham in the book of Genesis. In Acts, however, the promise is entirely associated with the Davidic covenant (see 2:29–33).[1] We have already seen Paul in 13:23 refer to how God brought forth Jesus, as a descendent of David, to bring salvation to Israel in fulfillment of the promise. Here too Paul invokes Israel's Scriptures that spoke of the Davidic king's enthronement as a means of interpreting Jesus's resurrection as his own heavenly enthronement (Ps 2:7; Isa 55:3; Ps 16:10). Thus, the fulfillment of the promise for the children comes about through "the raising up of Jesus" (13:32). This "raising up of Jesus" is what "has been written in the second Psalm" (13:33b), namely, God's enthronement of his Davidic Son to a position of rule in Zion. The most difficult part of Paul's speech is found in his citations of Isa 55:3 and Ps 16:10 in 13:34–35. The primary point here is that God's resurrection of Jesus from the dead is the act that unleashes the salvific blessings for Israel. Justification and forgiveness of sins is now available for those who submit to God's king, whereas those who fail to trust in him are warned of judgment (13:38–41).

1. I expand on Acts 13:32–37 in more detail in Jipp, "'For David Did Not Ascend,'" 50–54.

(2) PAUL'S GOSPEL FINDS A MIXED RECEPTION FROM THE SYNAGOGUE

Luke shows that Paul's gospel consistently provokes both acceptance and rejection in the Jewish synagogues. The paradigm for the Jews' mixed reaction to the gospel is seen in their response to Paul in Pisidian Antioch (13:42–52). On the one hand, after Paul's sermon many of the Jews "followed Paul and Barnabas" and listened to their message about "the grace of God" (13:43). On the other hand, when Paul and Barnabas show up the next Sabbath and find the "whole town assembled to hear the word of the Lord," a group of Jews are filled with jealousy and attack Paul and his message (13:44–45). What happens next provides a paradigm for Paul's preaching the gospel in the Jewish synagogue.

> Paul and Barnabas boldly replied, "It was necessary that the word of God be spoken to you first. Since you reject it and judge yourselves unworthy of eternal life, we are turning to the Gentiles." For this is what the Lord has commanded us: "I have made you a light for the Gentiles to bring salvation to the end of the earth." When the Gentiles heard this, they rejoiced and honored the word of the Lord, and all who had been appointed to eternal life believed. The word of the Lord spread through the whole region. But the Jews incited the prominent God-fearing women and the leading men of the city. They stirred up persecution against Paul and Barnabas and expelled them from their district. But Paul and Barnabas shook the dust off their feet against them and went to Iconium. And the disciples were filled with joy and the Holy Spirit. (13:46–52)

Paul's proclamation of the gospel seems to have resulted in *some level of acceptance* among the Jews in the synagogue. After all, Luke says in verse 44 that the entire town shows up to hear them proclaim the word of God and that it is when "the Jews" saw the great crowds that they were filled with jealousy. How should we understand Paul's response, which seems to interpret the event as the means whereby the gospel goes to the Gentiles (13:46b–47)? Is the Gentile mission contingent upon Jewish rejection of the gospel? If so, how would this fit with Paul's invocation of Isaiah to justify the turn to the Gentiles? We'll return to these questions in a moment.

We should note, however, that while we are expecting Paul now to move to the Gentiles completely and entirely, when he enters into Iconium Luke tells us that "they entered the Jewish synagogue *as was their usual practice* and spoke in such a way that a great number *of both Jews and Greeks believed* (14:1). Thus, whatever Paul's statement—"we are turning to the Gentiles" (13:47)—might mean, Acts certainly does not justify any conclusions that would suggest Paul no longer evangelizes the Jews. However, once again in Iconium, "unbelieving Jews" turn many of the Gentiles against the church (14:2). The gospel provokes conflict as the city is divided and some "side with the Jews and others with the apostles" and the apostles are forced out of Iconium again due to threats on their lives (14:5–7). After Paul and Barnabas preach in Lystra, the Jews who had opposed Paul in Pisidian Antioch and Iconium journey to Lystra and stir up the crowds with the result that they stone him, though he does not die (14:19).

In Paul's second missionary journey, with Silas, we have seen in our previous chapter that Paul once again consistently seeks to proclaim his gospel in the Jewish synagogue (16:11—18:23). Again, Luke reminds us that it was the usual custom or practice of Paul to proclaim the Messiah in the synagogue (e.g., 17:2). But ironically it is not the synagogue but the Gentile house that receives the gospel and becomes the base of operations for Paul's mission in each city: Lydia in Philippi (16:11–15, 40), the Philippian jailer (16:25–34), Jason in Thessalonica (17:6–7), and Titus Justus in Corinth (18:5–8). Throughout Paul's and Silas's missionary journey there is the continuing theme of a mixed reception among the Jews. So in Thessalonica some of the Jews "were persuaded and joined Paul and Silas" (17:4), but other Jews become jealous and attack the house of Jason where they are staying (17:5–7). The Jews in the Berean synagogue are of noble character and examine Paul's proclamation in light of the Scriptures with the result that "many of them believed" (17:12). Predictably, Jews from Thessalonica come to Berea and turn the crowds against Paul, forcing him to leave (17:12–15). In Corinth we find the mixed signals where Paul converts the head of the synagogue Crispus as well as his entire household (18:8), and yet we also find Paul's response to the Jews in the synagogue who resist Paul's proclamation: "[Paul] shook his clothes and told them, 'Your blood is now on your own heads! I am innocent. From now on I will go the Gentiles'" (18:6).

Interpretations of Luke's depiction of the Jewish people and the synagogue often have a difficult time maintaining the tension and complexity of the narrative. At this point, it is wise to resist over-interpretation or going beyond what Luke has said so far. What we have seen is that Paul's proclamation of the gospel has resulted in some limited positive reception from his Jewish audience. Not all Jews who hear Paul's proclamation of the Messiah are resistant to his message. But we have also seen that there is mounting opposition to Paul and his message. So much so, in fact, that almost every city has a group of Jews who are jealously and violently seeking to drive Paul out of their cities and regions. Despite the limited positive reception Paul's message has received, Paul has twice interpreted their rejection of him with harsh language of judgment and as the basis for his turn toward the Gentiles (13:46–47; 18:5–6).

(3) OPPOSITION TO PAUL IN JERUSALEM (21:10–40)

The violent opposition to Paul and his message is brought to a climax when Paul returns to Jerusalem. The reader of Luke's Gospel quickly gains the sense that this visit will mean trouble for Paul. Just as Jesus was divinely ordained to journey to Jerusalem and suffer the fate of a prophet (e.g., Luke 9:51–56), so Paul knows that God has ordained him to journey back to Jerusalem and declare that while he does not know what will happen there, "the Holy Spirit warns me that in every city that chains and afflictions are waiting for me" (Acts 20:23; cf. 19:21). Further, the prophet Agabus prophetically warns Paul that "the Jews in Jerusalem will bind" Paul and will "deliver him over to the Gentiles" (21:10–12), but Paul is resolute that he must go to Jerusalem even if it means his death (21:13–14). Luke is concerned here to demonstrate that just as Jesus journeyed to Jerusalem according to God's will, suffered, and was rejected by the Jewish leaders, so now the same thing is happening in Paul's journey to Jerusalem.[2] Just as the Jewish leaders rejected Jesus as the agent of God's visit of his people, so now again they are about to reject Paul and the second chance God had given them to accept God's salvation for his people. Luke also wants to show his readers that Paul (and by implication the Christian movement) is not a renegade

2. See Moessner, *Luke the Historian*, 264–69.

apostate Jew, but that the message of the resurrected Messiah is actually the fulfillment of God's promises to Israel in their own Scriptures. Paul is a faithful Israelite who believes and proclaims only what the OT Scriptures declare. This is the question that dominates Acts 21–26: Is Paul a faithful, Torah-observant Jew or is he a Jewish renegade?

On the one hand, we can give a simple answer to this question: Luke emphatically tell us, "Yes, Paul is a faithful Torah-observant Jew." First of all, we see that when Paul and his traveling mates arrive, "the Jerusalem brothers *welcomed* us warmly" (21:17). Second, when Paul declares how much success the mission is having among Gentiles, James and all the elders give praise to God (21:19–20a). In other words, they are fully supportive of Paul's mission to the Gentiles. Third, James's reminder that the Gentile believers need only to abide by the Jerusalem council's decree is a reaffirmation that Gentiles do not need to be circumcised or become Jews (21:25). Fourth, James simply assumes that Paul is faithful to the law in his desire to have Paul undergo a Nazarite vow so everyone will know that "you yourself observe and guard the Law" (21:24). The fact that all of these statements are coming from James, the head of the Jerusalem church, is further star witness testimony on Paul's behalf!

But we can see that this is certainly not everyone's opinion of Paul and that James's comments are offered precisely because some serious questions have been raised about Paul and his Gentile mission. We have seen that in almost every city where Paul has proclaimed the gospel, some Jews accept but many other Jews reject it and persecute Paul severely. Now as Paul enters into Jerusalem we see that he has become a huge problem, as James informs Paul, "You see, brother, how many thousands of Jews there are who have believed, and they are all zealous for the law. But they have been informed about you—that you are teaching all the Jews who are among the Gentiles to abandon Moses, telling them not to circumcise their children or to live according to our customs. So what is to be done? They will certainly hear that you have come" (21:20–22). James suggests that they make a public demonstration of Paul's obedience to the Torah by having him join some men who have taken a vow so "everyone will know that what they were told about you amounts to nothing, and that you yourself are also careful to observe the law" (21:24).

But when Paul enters into the Temple, we see that Jewish opposition to him crescendos in a remarkable way. The scene is incredibly similar to the riot that ensued over Paul's proclamation of the gospel in Ephesus. Both concern sacred temple space, as a group of Asian Jews claim that he has defiled the temple by bringing Greeks into the holy place (21:27–29). Paul's presence results in incredible riots, emphasized by Luke with the language of "mob," "riot," "confusion," and mob cries—"away with him" (21:30–36). There is a desire to do violence to Paul (21:31, 36). But perhaps the most important similarity can be seen in 21:28: "Fellow Israelites, help! This is the man who is teaching everyone everywhere against our people, our law, and this place; moreover, he has actually brought Greeks into the temple and has defiled this holy place." Now, on the one hand, one can simply reject this statement as false: Paul didn't bring Greeks into the holy place; he doesn't teach against the Jewish people, the law, and the temple. And from a certain standpoint, there is a lot of truth in this. James states that Paul is law-observant (21:24), Paul goes out of his way to have Timothy circumcised so as not to give offense to the Jews (16:1–5), and Luke explicitly tells the reader that the claim about Greeks entering the temple is false (21:29).

I suggest, however, that while we should indeed reject the accuracy of the claim in 21:28, we should try to understand why the claim is made. If Paul is indeed Torah-observant, faithful to the Jewish people, and not doing anything problematic with respect to the Temple, then *why do these Jews (and so many others) see him and his message as such a problem and a challenge to their way of life*? If Paul is faithful to his Jewish heritage, then why do Jews in every city become intensely angry with him and try to do away with him? Why, if Paul is loyal to Torah, do these Jews take three identity markers of their religion—people, law, and temple—and say that Paul is directly opposed to them?

I suggest that just as Paul's message of God's revelation in and through the crucified, resurrected, and exalted Lord Messiah challenged the Gentiles' entire way of life, being, and religion, so Paul's message of Jesus as the resurrected Messiah and his ensuing Gentile mission present a challenge to Judaism as well. In other words, Paul *is indeed* faithful to Judaism—to the people, to the Torah, and to the temple—but only in a way that is subordinate to his ultimate allegiance, namely, the resurrected Jewish Messiah around whom Paul has oriented his entire life. Stated another way, Paul's ultimate allegiance to the resurrected Messiah results in a radical reconfiguration of the meaning of his Jewish heritage and sacred Scriptures. In other words, chapters 21–26 are going to revolve around two ways of being faithful Jews: one that defines Judaism entirely around Torah and Temple, and one that defines faithfulness to Judaism as obedience to the resurrected Messiah Jesus. Thus, the Asian Jews are wrong: Paul is not a faithless apostate Jew who seeks to dispense with Israel's heritage. But there is certainly *some* truth in their claim: Paul's message claims that loyalty to Judaism ultimately resides in fidelity and allegiance to the Jewish Messiah, Jesus of Nazareth, who has been raised from the dead and exalted to God's right hand.

(4) PAUL'S DEFENSE SPEECHES BEFORE KINGS AND RULERS (CHS. 22–26)

To return to the plot, the Roman centurion rescues Paul from certain death at the hand of the mob in Jerusalem and incarcerates him (21:32–33). This begins a lengthy section of Acts where Paul is incarcerated and engaged in frequent defense speeches. Paul gives four defense speeches: 1) to the Jewish people (Acts 22:1–21); 2) to the Jewish chief priests and Sanhedrin (23:1–8); 3) to Felix, the Roman procurator of Judea (24:10–21); and 4) to King Herod Agrippa II (26:1–23). Rather than examine each one of these speeches, I will summarize the major themes. It is crucial to see that Paul does not preach the resurrected Jesus *instead* or *in replacement* of loyalty to his Jewish heritage or instead of loyalty to Judaism; rather, Paul argues that the true content of the Scriptures of Israel, true loyalty to his Jewish heritage, is found nowhere else than in confession of and obedience to the resurrected Messiah Jesus.

(a) Paul Is a Loyal, Faithful Jew

In Paul's first speech to the people in Jerusalem, the people take note when he speaks with his Hebrew dialect (22:2). He proclaims, "I am a Jewish man . . . raised and nurtured in this city, instructed at the feet of Gamaliel, with careful and accurate knowledge of the ancestral law, zealous for the law" (22:1–3). Paul repeatedly argues that he believes everything written in the law of Moses and the prophets (24:14–15). When he is on trial before Herod Agrippa II, we even see him asking the King, "Do you believe the prophets? I know that you believe" (26:27). No doubt Paul is going to claim that if he truly believes the prophets, then he will believe the resurrection. Also, a frequent refrain from the Roman governors is that Paul is innocent or at least has not done anything deserving of death (25:25–27). Throughout Acts 22–26 Paul argues that he has committed no crime, has not wronged his people or their traditions, and has nothing against the Jewish people in terms of a counter-accusation.

(b) Paul Is on Trial for the Hope of Israel, Namely, the Resurrection of the Dead

The narrative keeps suggesting that Paul is really on trial because of disputes over the Jewish law (18:14–15; 23:29), not because he is perceived to be a threat to Rome. God has visited his people by resurrecting the Messiah and has offered repentance and salvation in his name. And this is all in fulfillment of Jewish Scriptures. Thus, it is not simply "resurrection" that Paul proclaims, it is God's resurrection of Messiah Jesus. Paul states to Felix, then, that he "believes everything laid down according to the law or written in the prophets" and that this is the basis for his hope in the resurrection (24:14–15). He proclaims to Herod Agrippa II that his testimony regarding the suffering and resurrected Messiah is "what the prophets and Moses said would take place" (26:19–23). Again Paul states he is on trial "on account of my hope in the promise made by God to our ancestors, a promise that our twelve tribes hope to attain. . . . Why is it thought incredible by you that God raises the dead?" (26:6–8). When Paul says, in 26:22–23, that he is simply proclaiming that fulfillment of Moses and the prophets has taken place in the Messiah's suffering and resurrection from the dead, he is claiming that God has *now begun to fulfill and complete the promises he made to his people in their Scriptures*. The promised "age to come" has now arrived in the resurrection of the Messiah. The hope of Israel according to the Scriptures, Paul claims, is resurrection. God has raised Jesus from the dead; therefore, the hope of Israel and its promised blessings are here! Again, this is why, with the resurrection of Jesus, the salvific blessings are *now* available to God's people, including: the Holy Spirit (2:17–21, 30–33), the healing of the lame man (3:1–26), "salvation" (4:10–12), forgiveness of sins (5:30–31), and the blessings of justification and salvation (13:32–39).

We have seen repeatedly throughout Acts that the resurrected/exalted Messiah *in heaven* is able to be present with his church in a more powerful way from heaven precisely as the enthroned Messiah. And it is for this reason that "heaven" is consistently exerting influence on "earth" through the Spirit, signs and wonders, the angel of the Lord, and dreams/visions. So it should be no surprise that as Paul narrates "the hope of Israel," identified with the resurrected Messiah, he is consistently narrating *his own encounters with the heavenly, resurrected Jesus.* Thus, Paul re-narrates his encounter with "the great light from heaven" (22:7) and the resurrected Lord (22:6–11); Paul has, thereby, "seen the Righteous One and heard his voice" (22:14). Again, when he returns to the temple and is praying, Luke says "he saw Jesus, saying to me" (22:17–18). Later, after Paul's trial before the Sanhedrin, "the Lord stood near Paul and said, 'Keep up your courage! For just as you testified to me in Jerusalem, so you must bear witness also in Rome" (23:11). And then once more, Paul narrates his encounter with "the light from heaven, brighter than the sun" who is the Lord (26:12–18).

Again, Paul's emphasis is that he is on trial for the Messiah's resurrection, and that this event is the accomplishment of God's scriptural promises for the Jews. So strongly does Luke identify resurrection with the Jewish hope that the reader is led to view Paul as more faithful to his religion than the Jewish leaders who oppose it! Quite simply, Paul is on trial for "the hope of Israel" (28:20). Far from being a renegade who teaches against the Jewish people, Paul testifies to God's visit of the Jewish people through the resurrected Messiah. Paul's hope is for the people's acceptance of their visit from God (26:27–29), the opening of their eyes, their turn from darkness to light, and their inclusion into a people sanctified by faith (26:18).

So let's take one more look at the Asian Jews' claim: "This man teaches everyone everywhere against our people, our law, and this place" (21:28). Is it true that he teaches against "the Jewish people"? No, he characterizes his entire ministry as one of witness to them of the good news that God has sent his Messiah and raised him from the dead, and that this can result in the "opening of their eyes so that they may turn from darkness to light and from the power of Satan to God, so that they may receive forgiveness of sins and a place among those who are sanctified by faith in me" (26:18). Does he teach against the Torah? No! Paul characterizes the content of the Law and the Prophets as the resurrection of Israel's Messiah. But does he teach against the temple, as sacred space? There is nothing in his speeches that specifically addresses this issue (though see 21:17–26), but the one who accepts Paul's teaching must thereby confess that "the resurrected Messiah in heaven" is the one who now defines sacred space. God is not encountered or housed in temples—as both Paul (17:24–25) and Stephen have declared (7:48–50). God's supreme revelation is in heaven and is bound up with his Messiah who resides in heaven.

(5) A FINAL PORTRAIT OF PAUL THE MISSIONARY IN THE ENDING OF ACTS (27:1—28:31)

Acts 26 has concluded by heightening our expectations for Paul's appearance before Caesar (26:30–32), but instead Luke provides a lengthy description of Paul's sea voyage and shipwreck on Malta on the way to Rome (27:1—28:10) and Paul's appearance before the Jews in Rome (28:11–31). In order to fully understand a piece of literature, a movie, or a drama one must pay close attention to *how the story ends*. Where the narrator chooses to conclude the story, whether the conclusion fulfills or disrupts the reader's expectations for the story, and whether the conclusion produces closure or openness to the narrative, have enormous implications for one's overall understanding of the narrative. Good dramas and good pieces of literature do not end arbitrarily, but neither do they wrap everything up in a tidy way such that the reader doesn't reflect upon the ending of the story. Often a good ending to a story will bring closure to the narrative and will reinforce the entire story, giving it a sense of coherence, but it will also leave the reader wanting more, perhaps just a bit perplexed, and mulling over aspects of what's been encountered. In other words, stories frequently have both closure and openness.[3] We'll look at the ending of Acts in two parts, due to my belief that the first section is devoted to the theme of Paul and the Gentiles (27:1—28:10) and the second is focused upon the theme of Paul and the Jews (28:16–31).[4] I will focus especially upon how what we read in these final two chapters functions as an ending to

3. My own study here has benefited greatly from Troftgruben, *Conclusion Unhindered*; and Marguerat, *First Christian Historian*, chs. 7 and 10.

4. Much of what follows is a briefer and revised version of my more detailed argument in Jipp, *Divine Visitations*, 253–87.

the entire narrative of Acts and thereby produces closure and openness.

(a) Paul and the Gentiles: The Sea Voyage (27:1–44)

Luke spends a remarkable amount of time narrating Paul's sea voyage from Caesarea to Rome, fully complete with technical nautical terms. The scene is *incredibly long* and this causes a delaying effect, suggesting that the scene has some significance to it beyond simply telling us, "Paul made it successfully from point A to point B." Given that the reader is, at this point, expecting Paul's trial before Caesar and probably wondering about the verdict, this lengthy description of the sea voyage, I suggest, must have some literary and theological significance for Luke. We have seen that one of Luke's primary purposes in Acts is to describe how God's salvation has been sent to *both* Jew and Gentile through his witnesses, the major witness to the Gentiles obviously being Paul. But Luke has now spent almost six full chapters portraying Paul as engaged in an intra-Jewish debate, where he is giving defense speeches before Jews and Roman governors, rather than proclaiming the gospel to Gentiles. The narrative presents Paul as making no Gentile converts during his imprisonment, and this is a significant shift in the portrayal of Paul. So, when readers encounter Paul's final words in the narrative—"This salvation of God has been sent to the Gentiles" (Acts 28:28)—the closest narrative example they would have at hand to remind them of this fact would be Paul's final encounter with the elders of Ephesus, all the way back in Acts 20:17–35. Should Luke jump ahead to narrate the last scene of his story (Paul and the Jews in Rome), he risks the possibility of marginalizing the theme of God's salvation going to the Gentiles through Paul when he closes the book.

What we have, then, in 27:1—28:10 is a simultaneously realistic depiction of Paul's journey to Rome *and* a symbolic and open-ended depiction of Paul as God's powerful witness who offers salvation to the Gentiles. In other words, Luke uses the sea voyage and the episode on Malta to remind the readers that Paul is God's powerful witness, that he has been sent to take salvation to the Gentiles, and that the Gentiles are receptive, albeit in a symbolic, open manner. Let's look at the voyage in three headings.

First, ancient readers would recognize when they begin to read chapter 27 that they were in a *Greek-Hellenistic literary world*. In chapter 27 readers enter into the Hellenistic territory of sea travel adventures, storms, and shipwrecks. With Homer's *Odyssey* as the archetype and Vergil's *Aeneid* following suit, accounts of sea voyages were a favorite literary sub-genre for Hellenistic and Roman authors. The Mediterranean Sea was foundational to the culture and commerce of the Greeks and Romans. Thus, Luke's decision to devote forty-four verses to Paul's Mediterranean voyage marks a dramatic shift in the narrative setting, a shift into a setting that is markedly Hellenistic in orientation. The chapter is dominated by nautical terminology ("to set sail," Acts 27:2, 6, 24; "they beached the ship," Acts 27:41) and titles of the specific kinds of storms (such as "the wind called Euraquilo," Acts 27:14). Thus, both the theme of Mediterranean sea travel as well as the specific vocabulary signal that the reader is in Gentile territory.

Second, Luke characterizes Paul as a *Jesus-like witness*. On three occasions Luke presents Paul as intervening with prophecies, exhortations, and encouragements, thereby shaping Paul's character toward that of Jesus. In Paul's first intervention, while they are staying at Fair Havens (27:8), "Paul admonishes" (v. 9) the leaders of the ship to cease from continuing the journey because it will result in great destruction to the provisions, the ship, and the lives of those on board (v. 10). Luke shows Paul's prophecy being fulfilled when the ship encounters the typhoon Eraquilo and the sailors are forced to throw their provisions overboard (vv. 18–19). Luke's description of the storm and the hostile oceanic environment is vivid and the darkness is bleak: "neither sun nor stars gave any light for many days" (27:20a). The situation is so ghastly that Luke says, "All hope that we should be saved was taken away" (27:20b). Paul again comes to their aid with another prophetic word, this time a divine word of encouragement. Yes, they should have listened to Paul's first prophetic word, which, they are reminded, has now been fulfilled (27:21) as their ship has suffered great "damage and loss" (cf. 27:10), but now Paul exhorts them to be of good cheer (27:22). God's angel has visited Paul and promised that not one of those on board the ship will lose their life. Paul must appear before Caesar in Rome, and the angel has promised that "God will give to you all those who are sailing with you" (v. 24b). As God's prophet, Paul declares that everything will turn out as he has said (v. 25). Paul adds, however, one more prophecy and declares that they must run aground on an island (v. 26). On a third occasion, Paul exhorts (vv. 33–34) everyone to cease their fasting and nourish themselves with food for their own salvation (v. 34). Paul's breaking of bread is reminiscent of the practice of the early church in Acts (2:42–47; 4:32–35). And then, quoting a word from Luke's Jesus (Luke 21:18), Paul makes the promise that "not a hair from your head shall perish" (v. 34b). Based on this summary of Paul's three speaking interventions, we can claim that Luke characterizes Paul as a prophet. He makes prophecies that come to fulfillment (vv. 10–11, 21; v. 26; 28:1); he receives messages from God's angel and speaks on God's behalf (vv. 21–26); he quotes the words of Jesus (v. 34); he provides encouragement to his shipmates (vv. 33–37); and at no point does he appear distressed for he trusts in his God's providential ordering (vv. 25–26).

Third, Paul functions as an *agent of God's salvation* for his Gentile shipmates. Six times rescue from the sea is characterized with the same Greek word used for "salvation." As we have seen, the narrator notes that during the storm, "all hope that we should *be saved* was finally taken from us" (27:20b). When some of the sailors attempted to escape by leaving the ship, Paul warns the centurion, "If these men do not remain in the boat, you cannot *be saved*" (v. 31b). Paul's encouragement to his shipmates to eat is "for the purpose of *your salvation*" (v. 34). The centurion's decision to let the potentially escaping prisoners live is due to his desire "*to save* Paul" (v. 43a). And Paul's prophecy comes true when the ship runs aground safely on the island, and so the narrator adds, "and thus it happened that *all were saved* onto the land" (v. 44b; repeated again in 28:1). The Malta episode begins with a literary tie back to the salvation of the ship and all of the prisoners (28:1). While these texts are often translated with the word "safety" and while some ancient sea-voyage narratives do use the Greek word *soteria/sozo* to refer to the ship's safety, I suggest that the Lukan force of these words should be allowed to come through fully and should be translated, therefore, as "salvation." Note that Acts 27 also places an emphasis on the universality of salvation for "everyone" or "all persons" aboard the ship. Most important is the promise God makes to Paul that God "will freely give to you [Paul] all those sailing with you" (27:24). God's rescue of the ship through Paul is a metaphor for Gentile salvation. The salvation is God's, but Paul is the agent on whose behalf God acts and through whom God mediates this salvation. So, for example, Paul exhorts "everyone" to partake in the meal (27:33). Paul promises that "not one hair from your head shall perish" (27:34b). Again, in v. 35 Luke emphasizes that everyone partakes in eating the meal: "When [Paul] said these things, and had taken the bread he gave thanks to God before everyone and breaking it he began to eat." The narrator adds that "everyone" was encouraged by the meal (v. 36a), and that "everyone" in the ship numbered 276 persons (v. 37). While Acts 27:33–38 does not portray the Lord's Supper, the scene has strong sacramental overtones. Paul does exactly what Jesus does in terms of his taking the bread (Luke 9:16; 22:19), giving thanks to God (cf. Luke 9:16; 22:17, 19), breaking the bread (Luke 9:16; 22:19), and eating together (cf. Luke 22:15). But the meal also recalls the depiction of the Jerusalem community that engaged in "breaking the bread" (2:42), and when eating "received nourishment with joy and sincerity of heart" (2:46). Within Acts 27:33–38 Luke uses four variations of the phrase "to receive nourishment" (27:33, 34, 36, 38), suggesting that he intends Paul's meal to recall the early church's foundational act of breaking bread together. As the early church formed a family through sharing meals, so Paul and the prisoners are bound together as a community through sharing food. In sum, the similarity to the meal scenes in Luke's Gospel, the reference to salvation in v. 34, the portrayal of Paul as a prophet and agent of God's salvation, and the positive effect the meal has on the passengers suggests that Paul's meal with these Gentiles should be seen as a literary symbolization of Gentile salvation.

(b) Paul and the Gentiles II: Paul on Malta (28:1–10)

If in Acts 27 Paul continues the pattern of Jesus from the Gospel who extends divine and salvific hospitality as host to all people, in the Malta episode he is hospitably received as the guest who embodies the salvific and powerful presence of Jesus. The Malta episode operates according to the logic of a theoxeny, namely, hospitality to a deity. One typically finds the following three components: a) hospitality or inhospitality unwittingly bestowed by the host upon the journeying and disguised divine guest; b) a recognition scene where the divine identity of the visiting stranger is revealed to the host; and c) attendant rewards or retribution for the host based on their treatment of the god. Luke portrays the journeying Paul enacting the divine visit to Gentiles one final time in a memorable manner.

First, the barbarians show extraordinary hospitality to the shipwrecked Paul (28:1–2). Paul is a total stranger to the Maltese. The island contains no "brethren" (21:7–17; 28:12–15), no "friends" (27:3), and no synagogue with whom Paul can seek hospitality. The mention of a story of sailors who shipwreck on an unfamiliar island activates an impending *inhospitality* scenario for ancient readers. Shipwrecked strangers were entirely vulnerable and at the mercy of those they encounter. This is exemplified well by Odysseus in the *Odyssey* who, when encountering a new land in his voyage, utters the stock phrase: "Alas, to the land of what mortals have I now come? Are they insolent, wild, and unjust? Or are they hospitable to strangers and fear the gods in their thoughts?" (Homer, *Odyssey* 6.119–21). And Luke's use of the term "barbarian" activates resonances of non-Greeks who are uncivilized and inhospitable, like Polyphemus the Cyclops! Yet Luke overturns this negative stereotype of "the barbarian" by the glowing statement: "the barbarians showed us no insignificant kind humanity." This is exactly the kind of virtue one would not expect from "barbarians"! Luke expands on the barbarians' noble behavior by stating that "they hospitably received all of us by lighting a fire because of the pouring rain and the cold" (28:2b). The Maltese's bestowal of hospitality upon Paul and the crew is the height of virtue, given that these "strangers" have no means for reciprocating.[5]

Second, Paul's identity, as one who embodies the powerful presence of Jesus, is revealed to the barbarians in his victory over the viper (28:3–6). Through Paul's successful encounter with the viper wherein he is unharmed by and destroys the serpent, Paul is revealed to be an agent of Jesus who defeats evil in new territories wherever he journeys. Both the reaction of the Maltese, namely that this attacked prisoner will die (28:4), and the symbolic valences of vipers within Luke-Acts as agents of evil (Luke 3:7; 10:18–19; 11:11–12), demonstrate that the viper is an enemy of Paul. The barbarians' acclamation that Paul is a god, then, is not altogether incorrect, since they rightly recognize Paul's embodiment of divine power (i.e., the presence of Jesus). Their inaccurate exclamation in verse 4 thereby functions as a foil to be overturned by the ensuing event, which accurately reveals Paul's identity: "then, however, he shook off the beast into the fire and he suffered no evil" (28:5). Paul's "suffering no evil" marks him as God's emissary and is the result of Jesus's promise that nothing, including serpents and scorpions, shall be able to harm his disciples (Luke 10:19). As Jesus's emissary, Paul demonstrates the success of the powerful divine visitation precisely through his immunity to *and* destruction of the deadly creature. These successful encounters over "serpents and scorpions" function as demonstrations of Satan's destruction through Jesus's emissaries (e.g., Acts 8:14–24; 13:4–12; 16:16–18; 19:11–20). Every reader of Acts knows that their exclamation is theologically imprecise as Luke has often enough corrected the pagan predilection to blur the boundaries of humans

5. On Luke's subversion of negative ethnic and cultural stereotyping in Acts, see Jipp, "Hospitable Barbarians," 23–45. With respect to overturning negative stereotypes of Roman centurions, see Brink, *Soldiers in Luke-Acts.*

and gods (e.g., Acts 10:25–26; 14:8–19), but there is much to commend in the barbarians' perception of Paul. Paul's immunity to the snake, whereby he conquers the demonic, demonstrates that Jesus's resurrection power is at work in Paul and that he is marked as God's emissary.

Third, Paul bestows gifts of healing to the Maltese, and the relationship between Paul and the Maltese is cemented through further hospitality (28:7–10). The barbarians' recognition of Paul's identity, demonstrated through his power over death and defeat of the serpent (28:3–6), is appropriately followed by the extraordinary hospitality of "Publius the first man of the island" (28:7a). Publius's impulse to heighten and continue the Maltese's hospitality to Paul functions as a confirmation of the Maltese's full acceptance of Paul. We have seen that Gentile hospitality to the travelling missionaries of the gospel is one of the primary right responses to them and the gospel message. The gospel takes root in new lands through hospitable households that welcome God's witnesses. Publius's hospitality thereby functions as the total reception of Paul as God's witness. It is, therefore, no surprise that Paul reciprocates Publius's hospitality through the gift of healing (28:9b). The hospitable treatment of Paul results, then, in the healing of both Publius's father (28:8) as well as all the rest of the islanders suffering from sicknesses and diseases (28:9). The episode concludes by returning to the Maltese's extraordinary hospitality to Paul and the crew: "they bestowed many honors upon us and as we were setting sail they placed on board the things we needed" (28:10). The language refers to the Maltese's sharing of possessions and the things needed for the voyage.

The Malta episode (Acts 28:1–10) is, therefore, *the final and climactic successful episode* of the manifestation of the salvific divine visitation in new Gentile territory,

the revelation of Paul's identity as the powerful agent of
Jesus, and the total acceptance of the divine visit through
Gentile hospitality, which results in their incorporation
into the new fictive kinship group. The Maltese are idyllic
hosts; they recognize the divine power at work in Paul and
respond with hospitality; they are philanthropic in their
treatment of shipwrecked strangers; and they know how to
initiate guest-friendship with the agent of the divine visit.
The episode functions for the reader as a final and memorable reminder of the success of the salvific divine visitation
among hospitable Gentiles.

(c) Paul and the Roman Jews (28:16–31)

Paul's final encounter with the Jewish leaders in Rome
in 28:16–31 contrasts sharply with what we have seen in
27:1—28:10, and we are returned to the defense speeches
from chapters 22–26. The scene is a familiar one. First,
Paul is again portrayed as God's emissary to the Jews. In
28:17–20 Paul recounts his faithful witness to Israel. Paul
declares to them, and reminds us again, that he is loyal to
the Jewish people and their customs (28:17b), that he has
no counter-accusation to make against his people (28:19),
and that his chains are evidence of his devotion to "the hope
of Israel" (28:20). The Roman Jews declare that they have
heard nothing evil about Paul and invite him to declare his
views (28:21–22). Paul spends night and day "testifying
about the kingdom of God" and seeking to "persuade them
about Jesus from both the Law of Moses and the Prophets"
(28:23).

Second, there is once again a mixed response to
Paul's proclamation from the Roman Jews. Luke declares
that "some were persuaded by what he said, but others did
not believe" (28:24). Paul concludes with a long quotation

from Isa 6, which both highlights Paul's role as an Isaiah-like prophet whose testimony is rejected *and* functions as a rebuke of Jewish unbelief (28:25–27). While there is no reason to deny that Luke portrays some Jews as genuinely persuaded by Paul's proclamation, the heightened intensity of the scene indicates that Luke intends the reader to view Paul's preaching as a failure. Paul's proclamation results in "disunity" among the Jewish people (28:25), which stands in contrast to the unity of the witness of Paul, Isaiah, and the Spirit who all agree in their "one word" of judgment against the Jews: "Paul spoke *one word*, 'Rightly did the Holy Spirit speak through the Prophet Isaiah to your fathers.'" The Jews in Rome thereby join the ranks of the Jews in Pisidian Antioch (13:44–52) and Corinth (18:5–6) as they reject Paul's gospel. The Roman Jews' inability to "see" the salvation of God is tragic given Luke's narration of the restoration of Israel (see ch. 3; cf. Luke 2:30).

Finally, the conclusion to Acts contains elements of both narratival openness and closure. In many ways, Paul's arrival in Rome and his proclamation to the Roman Jews does fulfill narrative expectations (e.g., 23:11; 27:24–26); Paul's opening remarks summarize in quick fashion what has taken place in the preceding seven chapters; the Jews' rejection of Paul's gospel is the third and representative scene of Paul's inability to persuade the Jewish leaders of the gospel; and the weight of Paul's invocation of Isa 6 as judgment seems to close the door on the narrative's hope of fully persuading the Jewish people of Jesus as the Messiah. But there are also strong notes of openness. Three in particular are obvious. First, we never hear of Paul's trial before Caesar or Paul's anticipation of his death (e.g., 20:23–25; 21:13; 23:11). Second, the final words of Acts leave the ongoing story of Paul and the proclamation of the gospel to the reader's imagination: "Paul stayed two whole years in his own rented house. And he welcomed all who visited him, proclaiming the kingdom of God and teaching about the Lord Jesus Christ with all boldness and without hindrance" (28:30–31). Third, Paul's final words—"The salvation of God has been sent to the Gentiles; they will listen" (28:28)—especially in light of Paul's recent favorable interactions with Gentiles in Malta, suggest an ongoing and expanding mission to the Gentiles that exceeds the pages of Acts.

REFLECTION

1. Why did Paul provoke hostility from many among the Jewish people? Would it be fair to say that Paul was an opponent or a threat to Judaism?

2. What does the sea voyage in chapter 27 contribute to the story of Acts?

8

READING ACTS AS THE PEOPLE OF GOD

A Brief Postscript

THERE ARE A VARIETY of reasons—many of them good ones—why one might be compelled to read Acts. But, of course, the main reason why people continue to read and care about the book of Acts is because it is Christian Scripture and, therefore, makes theological claims about the Christian God, the church, and the meaning of human life. Given that Acts witnesses to a God once engaged and *still engaged* within history to accomplish his purposes, to a reign of the resurrected and exalted Messiah that spans the apostolic age and into *our* age, and to the Holy Spirit who *once and still* mediates divine knowledge and power to the believer, anyone who reads is invited to understand his or her own life, will, and history in continuity with the history and theology of Acts.[1] The book of Acts constantly claims to describe the reader's own human situation and need for God, and so the reader of Acts is constantly pressed to engage in asking: what does this text, statement, claim mean

---

1. I repeat here a small portion of my argument, and one influenced by Adolf Schlatter, in Jipp, "Beginnings of a Theology." See here also Rowe, *World Upside Down*, 174.

for me, for humanity? Reading Acts is, then, inherently self-involving as it summons the reader to believe, confess, obey, and understand the entirety of one's existence—both one's thinking and willing—in light of the God revealed in the text.

Furthermore, the narrative of Acts creates a world that is universalizing in that its vision claims to constitute the world of the reader. Given that the subject matter of Acts is the one God who has intervened within history through Jesus to fulfill the promises he made to Israel, and for the salvation of the world, the narrative makes a totalizing claim upon its readers. The world that is created by the story of Acts, in this instance, claims to define all of reality, the situation of all of humanity, and all of our human experiences. I think that it is appropriate, then, having examined the major features of the narrative of Acts, to conclude with a very brief look at some of the essential features of the identity and core practices of the church in Acts as a means of stimulating theological reflection for contemporaries who read Acts as the Word of God.

(1) THE IDENTITY OF THE CHURCH

(a) The Continuing Significance of Israel

We have seen that God has been faithful to the promises he made to his people, Israel. God did not turn his back upon his people when he brought the church into existence. The mission to Israel contained elements of both success and disappointment. Even Paul's ministry to Israel in the synagogue, fraught with difficulties, persecution, and rejection though it was, resulted in some of the Jewish people turning to Jesus as Israel's Messiah. Acts is not a supersessionist text such that space is made for the Gentiles through Israel's rejection. Gentile believers in Jesus are incorporated, then, by virtue of their connection to the Messiah, into the history of Israel and God's continued dealings with his people.[2]

(b) The Resurrection and Heavenly Enthronement of the Messiah

God's resurrection and enthronement of the Davidic Messiah has placed this Jesus in a position of power to rule over his people. Acts portrays the risen Jesus as continuing to communicate with his people through dreams and visions, as vindicating his righteous and faithful ones, sending forth salvific blessings and times of spiritual refreshment, moving his witnesses forward in their mission, and pouring out his Spirit upon his people. The name of Jesus is powerful to heal and restore, to conquer evil, and to create transformed, repentant lives. The resurrected Messiah is, further, the one endowed with God's authority to judge the entire world. The enthroned Messiah, then, is physically absent but continues to be powerfully present with his people.

(c) The Church Is a Multiethnic People Engaged in Mission

As Peter had declared, this Jewish Messiah is "Lord of *all*" (10:36). He is the Lord of Israel, but he is also the Lord of all the varieties of ethnicities and peoples that populate the pages of Acts. The gift of the Spirit, which is the defining feature of the Messiah's heavenly rule, is the great equalizer that functions to include Jews, Samaritans, and all the pagan peoples as belonging to God.[3] The Spirit is the Spirit of cross-cultural testimony who enables people to cross

2. One of the most significant theological treatments of this theme, and one conducive for reflection upon the book of Acts, is Jennings, *Christian Imagination*. See now his commentary, Jennings, *Acts*.

3. For powerful reflections upon the role of the Spirit in Acts and contemporary mission, see Yong, *Hospitality and the Other*.

geographical boundaries and transgress cultural stigmas in order to share the gospel with others. Negative stereotypes of Samaritans, eunuchs, and barbarians are not a good gauge for understanding real humans, and Acts frequently subverts these stereotypes by showing all people as capable of virtue and a right response to the gospel. For this reason, one of the most obvious features of the church is that it is engaged in mission. The main characters travel thousands of miles in order to take the gospel to new peoples and to ensure that the established churches remain committed to Christ in their church life.

(d) The Church Is Central to God's Purposes

It is so obvious that some might overlook the fact that God stands behind the creation and existence of the church as well as its establishment even against powerful people and governments that oppose it. Throughout Acts the church has enemies, most external but some internal, who seek to destroy it. Judas, as one of the Twelve, threatened to undo God's restoration of Israel. Ananias and Sapphira represent a serious threat to the unity of the church and its common life. The Jewish leaders and Sanhedrin, Herod Agrippa I, and the governing authorities in Philippi all attempt to stop the movement through incarcerating its leaders. In every instance, God providentially ensures that the church is established despite suffering and opposition. We might add here the way in which God initiates the movement of the gospel into new territories such that the growth of the church is a divine act. Thus, God is the one who sends visions and angels to Cornelius and Peter so that the gospel can move freely to Gentiles; God sends a vision to Paul and Silas to force them into Macedonia; and God providentially protects Paul on the ship so that he can make it to Malta and Rome.

(2) THE PRACTICES OF THE CHURCH

(a) Allegiance to the Messiah

Acts offers a variety of necessary human responses that demonstrate allegiance to God's resurrected and en-throned-in-heaven messianic king.[4] One of the most basic responses here is captured with the traditional Christian language of faith, repentance, and baptism. For example, after Peter's sermon about God's resurrection of the Messiah, Luke recounts the following about the people: "When they heard this, they were pierced to the heart and said to Peter and the rest of the apostles, 'Brothers, what should we do?' Peter replied, 'Repent and be baptized, each of you, in the name of Jesus Christ'" (2:37–38a). The power of faith in Jesus Christ is exemplified in the next narrative where the lame man is healed and receives the messianic bless-ings by "faith in his name" (3:16). The power of the risen Lord is consistently demonstrated throughout the narrative by signs and wonders, the ability to heal through his emis-saries, and the creation of a transformed repentant people. The centrality of faith toward Jesus Christ is demonstrated in the Jerusalem council where there is the repeated refrain of God cleansing the Gentiles through faith (15:6–11). It is not accidental, then, that the first Gentile Paul encoun-ters on his mission after the Jerusalem council is spoken of as having faith in the Lord and being baptized (16:15). Faith, repentance (17:30), and baptism (8:36–38) are acts

4. On the use of the language of allegiance to describe the ap-propriate response to the crucified and risen Messiah in Paul's letters, see Bates, *Salvation as Allegiance Alone*.

that convey a turning away from one's prior allegiances and instead now display loyalty toward Christ.

(b) Testimony to the Messiah

One can hardly fail to notice the remarkable emphasis Luke places on verbal proclamation of the gospel, not least in light of the frequency of apostolic speeches throughout the book. At key points in the narrative, Luke speaks of the Word of God as an active agent: "the Word of God became great and multiplied" (6:7; cf. 12:24; 19:20). The primary function of the major characters in Acts is to be "witnesses" (1:8; 5:32; 22:15). They have experienced God's incredible act of raising the crucified Messiah from the dead, and therefore their primary responsibility is to testify to what God has done. The apostles are unable to keep quiet about what God has done despite repeated commands from the Jewish Sanhedrin, and God continues to empower the witnesses for bold proclamation through the gift of the Holy Spirit (4:23–31; 5:31–32). God's witnesses, however, do not only testify to what God *has done*, they are required to remain attentive to what God *is doing*. We have seen how the human characters discern God's activity throughout the narrative. The most obvious example of this is Peter's discernment that God had included the Gentiles within God's people and had cleansed their hearts by faith.

(c) Hospitality to Strangers

We have seen that one of the primary and appropriate Gentile responses to God's messengers is hospitality. Lydia, the Philippian jailer, Jason, Titius Justus, and Publius all respond to Paul with welcome into their homes. Cornelius receives Peter and thereby the gospel message into his

Gentile house. This accords with a book that seeks to show the universality of the gospel message, that Jesus is "Lord of all" (10:36), and that there is indeed no partiality with God (10:34). This is of one piece with the frequent undercutting of ancient stereotypes: barbarians are not inhospitable to Paul (28:1–10); Samaritans respond with joy to the gospel (8:4–17); and eunuchs readily respond to the Christological proclamation of the Scriptures (8:26–40).

(d) The Unity of the Church

Readers of Acts will almost certainly be struck by the common life of the early church and its incredible display of unity. Luke's summaries of the Jerusalem community emphasize its unity, devotion to one another through sharing possessions, and their taking meals together (2:42–47; 4:32–35). The church functions as a community of friends that remains devoted to one another even in spite of external and internal threats to their common life (e.g., 4:1–22; 5:1–11; 6:1–6).

While much more could be said about the identity and practices of the church, these are offered as a means of stimulating the imaginations and thoughts of those who read Acts as Christian Scripture. I suspect that Luke hoped his account of the rise and expansion of the earliest church would produce confidence and renewed faith and allegiance in the God who had acted to bring into existence a worldwide, multiethnic family of people who were loyal to King Jesus and who sought to pattern their lives and churches in ways that bear continuity with the identity and practices of the church that dot the pages of Acts.

REFLECTION

1. Why do you read the book of Acts? What value does reading it have for you?

2. What practices of the church would you add to the list? Do any of the practices seem to you to need recovery in the life of the church?

BIBLIOGRAPHY

Adams, Sean A. *The Genre of Acts and Collected Biography*. Society for New Testament Studies Monograph Series 156. Cambridge: Cambridge University Press, 2013.

Alexander, Loveday. *The Preface to Luke's Gospel: Literary Convention and Social Context in Luke 1.1–4 and Acts 1.1*. Society for New Testament Studies Monograph Series 78. Cambridge: Cambridge University Press, 1993.

Anderson, Kevin L. *"But God Raised Him from the Dead": The Theology of Jesus's Resurrection in Luke-Acts*. Paternoster Biblical Monographs. London: Paternoster, 2006.

Barreto, Eric D. *Ethnic Negotiations: The Function of Race and Ethnicity in Acts 16*. WUNT 2.294. Tübingen: Mohr-Siebeck, 2010.

Bates, Matthew. *Salvation as Allegiance Alone: Rethinking Faith, Works, and the Gospel of King Jesus*. Grand Rapids: Baker Academic, 2017.

Bonz, Marianne Palmer. *The Past as Legacy: Luke-Acts and Ancient Epic*. Minneapolis: Fortress, 2000.

Brink, Laurie. *Soldiers in Luke-Acts: Engaging, Contradicting, and Transcending the Stereotypes*. WUNT 2.362. Tübingen: Mohr-Siebeck, 2014.

Fitzmyer, Joseph A. "David, 'Being Therefore a Prophet . . . ' (Acts 2:30)." *Catholic Biblical Quarterly* 34 (1972) 332–39.

Frei, Hans W. *The Identity of Jesus Christ*. Eugene, OR: Wipf & Stock, 1997.

Gaventa, Beverly R. *Acts*. Abingdon New Testament Commentaries. Nashville: Abingdon, 2003.

————. *From Darkness to Light: Aspects of Conversion in the New Testament*. Overtures to Biblical Theology. Minneapolis: Fortress, 1986.

González, Justo L. *The Story Luke Tells: Luke's Unique Witness to the Gospel*. Grand Rapids: Eerdmans, 2015.

Goswell, Greg. "The Order of the Books of the New Testament." *Journal of the Evangelical Theological Society* 55 (2010) 225–41.

Green, Joel B. "Internal Repetition in Luke-Acts: Contemporary Narratology and Lucan Historiography." In *History, Literature, and Society in the Book of Acts*, edited by Ben Witherington III, 283–99. Cambridge: Cambridge University Press, 1996.

———. "The Problem of a Beginning: Israel's Scriptures in Luke 1–2." *Bulletin for Biblical Research* 4 (1994) 61–86.

Haenchen, Ernst. *The Acts of the Apostles: A Commentary*. Louisville: Westminster John Knox, 1971.

Holladay, Carl R. *Acts: A Commentary*. The New Testament Library. Louisville: Westminster John Knox, 2016.

Hurtado, Larry W. *Destroyer of the Gods: Early Christian Distinctiveness in the Roman World*. Waco: Baylor University Press, 2016.

Jennings, Willie James. *Acts*. Belief: A Theological Commentary on the Bible. Louisville: Westminster John Knox, 2017.

———. *The Christian Imagination: Theology and the Origins of Race*. New Haven: Yale University Press, 2010.

Jervell, Jacob. "The Divided People of God: The Restoration of Israel and Salvation for the Gentiles." In *Luke and the People of God: A New Look at Luke-Acts*, by Jacob Jervell, 41–74. Minneapolis: Augsburg Fortress, 1972.

———. *Luke and the People of God: A New Look at Luke-Acts*. Minneapolis: Augsburg Fortress, 1972.

———. *The Theology of the Acts of the Apostles*. New Testament Theology. Cambridge: Cambridge University Press, 1996.

———. "The Twelve on Israel's Thrones: Luke's Understanding of the Samaritans in Luke-Acts." In *Luke and the People of God: A New Look at Luke-Acts*, by Jacob Jervell, 75–112. Minneapolis: Augsburg Fortress, 1972.

Jipp, Joshua W. "The Beginnings of a Theology of Luke-Acts: Divine Activity and Human Response." *Journal of Theological Interpretation* 8 (2014) 23–43.

———. *Divine Visitations and Hospitality to Strangers in Luke-Acts: An Interpretation of the Malta Episode in Acts 28:1–10*. Supplements to Novum Testamentum 153. Leiden: Brill, 2013.

———. "'For David Did Not Ascend into Heaven . . . ' (Acts 2:34a): Reprogramming Royal Psalms to Proclaim the Enthroned-in-Heaven King." In *Ascent Into Heaven in Luke-Acts: New Explorations of Luke's Narrative Hinge*, edited by David K. Bryan and David W. Pao, 41–60. Minneapolis: Fortress, 2016.

———. "Hospitable Barbarians: Ethnic Reasoning in Acts 28:1–10," *Journal of Theological Studies* 68 (2017) 23–45.

———. "Luke's Scriptural Suffering Messiah: A Search for Precedent, a Search for Identity." *The Catholic Biblical Quarterly* 72 (2010) 255–74.

Bibliography

———. "Paul's Areopagus Speech of Acts 17:16–34 as *Both* Critique *and* Propaganda." *Journal of Biblical Literature* 131 (2012) 567–88.

Johnson, Luke Timothy. *The Acts of the Apostles.* Sacra Pagina 5. Collegeville, MN: Liturgical, 1992.

———. *Scripture and Discernment: Decision Making in the Church.* Nashville: Abingdon, 1996.

Keener, Craig S. *Acts: An Exegetical Commentary.* 4 Vols. Grand Rapids: Baker Academic, 2012–15.

Marguerat, Daniel. *The First Christian Historian: Writing the "Acts of the Apostles."* Society for New Testament Studies Monograph Series 121. Cambridge: Cambridge University Press, 2002.

Matson, David L. *Household Conversion Narratives in Acts: Pattern and Interpretation.* The Library of New Testament Studies 123. Sheffield: Sheffield Academic Press, 1996.

Minear, Paul S. *To Heal and to Reveal: The Prophetic Vocation according to Luke.* New York: Seabury, 1976.

Moessner, David Paul. *Luke the Historian of Israel's Legacy, Theologian of Israel's "Christ": A New Reading of the "Gospel Acts" of Luke.* Beihefte zur Zeitschrift für die neutestamentliche Wissenschaft 182. Boston: De Gruyter, 2016.

Mowery, Robert L. "Lord, God, and Father: Theological Language in Luke-Acts." *Society of Biblical Literature Seminar Papers* (1995) 82–101.

Padilla, Osvaldo. *The Acts of the Apostles: Interpretation, History and Theology.* Downers Grove, IL: InterVarsity, 2016.

Pao, David W. *Acts and the Isaianic New Exodus.* Wissenschaftliche Untersuchungen zum Neuen Testament 2/130. Tübingen: Mohr Siebeck, 2000.

Parsons, Mikeal C. *Acts.* Paideia Commentaries on the New Testament. Grand Rapids: Baker Academic, 2008.

Parsons, Mikeal C., and Richard I. Pervo. *Rethinking the Unity of Luke and Acts.* Minneapolis: Fortress, 1993.

Pervo, Richard I. *Profit with Delight: The Literary Genre of the Acts of the Apostles.* Minneapolis: Fortress, 1987.

Powell, Mark Allan. *What Is Narrative Criticism?* Minneapolis: Fortress, 1991.

Rothschild, Clare K. *Luke-Acts and the Rhetoric of History.* WUNT 2.175. Tübingen: Mohr-Siebeck, 2004.

Rowe, Kavin C. "History, Hermeneutics and the Unity of Luke-Acts." *Journal for the Study of the New Testament* 28 (2005) 131–57.

Bibliography

———. *World Upside Down: Reading Acts in the Graeco-Roman Age.* Oxford: Oxford University Press, 2009.

Schnabel, Eckhard J. *Acts.* Zondervan Exegetical Commentary on the New Testament 5. Grand Rapids: Zondervan 2012.

Scott, James M. "Luke's Geographical Horizon." In *The Book of Acts in Its First Century Setting.* Vol. 2, *The Book of Acts in Its Graeco-Roman Setting,* edited by David W. J. Gill and Conrad Gempf, 483–544. Grand Rapids: Eerdmans, 1994.

Shauf, Scott. *The Divine in Acts and in Ancient Historiography.* Minneapolis: Fortress, 2015.

Skinner, Matthew L. *Intrusive God, Disruptive Gospel: Encountering the Divine in the Book of Acts.* Grand Rapids: Brazos, 2015.

Sleeman, Matthew. *Geography and the Ascension Narrative in Acts.* Society for New Testament Studies Monograph Series 146. Cambridge: Cambridge University Press, 2013.

Smith, David E. *The Canonical Function of Acts: A Comparative Analysis.* Collegeville, MN: Liturgical, 2002.

Squires, John T. *The Plan of God in Luke-Acts.* Society for New Testament Studies Monograph Series 76. Cambridge: Cambridge University Press 1993.

Stark, Rodney. *The Rise of Christianity: How the Obscure, Marginal Jesus Movement Became the Dominant Religious Force in the Western World in a Few Centuries.* Princeton: Princeton University Press, 1996.

Sterling, Gregory E. "'Opening the Scriptures': The Legitimation of the Jewish Diaspora and the Early Christian Mission." In *Jesus and the Heritage of Israel: Luke's Narrative Claim upon Israel's Legacy,* edited by David P. Moessner, 199–217. Harrisburg, PA: Trinity Press International, 1999.

Strauss, Mark. *The Davidic Messiah in Luke-Acts: The Promise and Its Fulfillment in Lukan Christology.* The Library of New Testament Studies 110. Sheffield: Sheffield Academic Press, 1995.

Talbert, Charles H. *Literary Patterns, Theological Themes, and the Genre of Luke-Acts.* Society of Biblical Literature Monograph Series 20. Missoula, MT: Society of Biblical Literature, 1974.

Tannehill, Robert C. *The Narrative Unity of Luke-Acts: A Literary Interpretation.* Vol. 2, *The Acts of the Apostles.* Minneapolis: Augsburg Fortress, 1990.

Thompson, Alan J. *The Acts of the Risen Lord Jesus: Luke's Account of God's Unfolding Plan.* New Studies in Biblical Theology 27. Downers Grove, IL: IVP Academic, 2011.

Bibliography

Troftgruben, Troy M. *A Conclusion Unhindered: A Study of the Ending of Acts within Its Literary Environment.* Wissenschaftliche Untersuchungen zum Neuen Testament 2/280. Tübingen: Mohr Siebeck, 2010.

VanderKam, James C. "The Festival of Weeks and the Story of Pentecost in Acts 2." In *From Prophecy to Testament: The Function of the Old Testament in the New*, edited by Craig A. Evans, 185–205. Peabody, MA: Hendrickson, 2004.

Wall, Robert W. "The Acts of the Apostles in Canonical Context." *Biblical Theology Bulletin* 18 (1988) 16–24.

Weaver, John B. *Plots of Epiphany: Prison-Escape in Acts of the Apostles.* Beihefte zur Zeitschrift für die neutestamentliche Wissenschaft und die Kunde der älteren Kirche 131. Berlin: Walter de Gruyter, 2004.

Wendel, Susan J. *Scriptural Interpretation and Community Self-Definition in Luke-Acts and the Writings of Justin Martyr.* Supplements to Novum Testamentum 139. Leiden: Brill, 2011.

Wilson, Brittany E. *Unmanly Men: Refigurations of Masculinity in Luke-Acts.* Oxford: Oxford University Press, 2015.

Yong, Amos. *Hospitality and the Other: Pentecost, Christian Practices, and the Neighbor.* Maryknoll, NY: Orbis, 2008.

SUBJECT INDEX

Abrahamic Promises, 33,
56, 67, 78, 108

Acts (book of)
    authorship, 2
    genre, 3–9
    purpose, 122
    relationship to Luke's
        Gospel, 10–12, 31,
        43, 49, 78, 108

Church
    growth, 1, 9, 18, 22, 136
    relationship to Israel,
        15, 35, 62–63, 65–
        66, 82–83, 134–35
    protection by God,
        21–22, 27, 105

David
    Psalms of, 19–20, 28, 44
    throne of, 32, 43, 70,
        73–74, 83, 98,
        107–8, 135

forgiveness of sin, 16, 58,
    67, 119, 120

gentiles
    mission to, 22–23, 38,
        56, 136–37
    inclusion in the people
        of God, 67, 78–85,
        86–105

God
    oneness, 17, 95, 101,
        133, 134
    plans of, 23–24, 37–38,
        53, 78–79, 87–88,
        104, 113, 133, 138
    superiority over idols,
        97–99

hospitality, 49, 79, 80,
    88–93, 126–130,
    138–139

Israel
    election, 52, 67, 107
    restoration of, 33–34,
        39–40, 48, 50, 55,
        67, 68–69, 84, 131,
        136

Kingdom of God, 12,
    34–38, 40, 97–99,
    102, 132

Messiah
    relationship to Israel's
        history, 16, 31–32,
        118–19
    resurrection of, 44–45,
        52, 55, 57, 58, 70,
        87, 93, 95, 106, 108,
        118–20, 135

Messiah (*continued*)

rejection of, 47, 53, 59, 62, 64, 92–93, 110, 112–13

exaltation of, 43, 46–47, 55, 64, 65, 119

as a descendant of David, 32–33, 36, 42–44, 52, 55, 70, 108

mission, 38, 40, 52, 60–62, 67, 71, 72, 86–105, 135–36

possessions, 19, 48, 49, 70, 90, 97, 99, 139

repentance, 36, 47, 47–50, 53–56, 62, 70, 73, 109, 120, 137–38

Scripture

interpretation of, 27–28, 53, 56, 80, 116–17

fulfillment of, 32–40, 50, 53–55, 59, 62, 74, 75–76, 78, 80, 109, 114, 118–19

Spirit

as a means of interpretation, 26, 53, 80

empowerment by, 35, 42, 52, 58, 60, 68

reception of, 40–42, 46, 49, 52, 70, 73

SCRIPTURE INDEX

OLD TESTAMENT

Genesis
10	68, 69
11	69
12:1–4	33, 67
18:9–15	32
22:18	56
49:8–12	32

Exodus
19:16–18	41

Leviticus
19:15–19	80
21:16–23	75
23:29	55

Deuteronomy
6:4	17
6:5	18
10:17–19	80
16:9–12	41
18:15	63
18:15–18	49, 55
23:1	75
34:9–11	49

1 Samuel
1–2	32

2 Samuel
7:12	12
7:12–14	107
22:51	107

1 Kings
12:16–20	72
16:24	72

2 Kings
17:24	72

1 Chronicles
17	32
17:4–14	107

Psalms
2	32
2:1–3	59
2:7	109
15	44, 45
15:9–10	44
15:11	45
16:10	109
17	43
69:1–4	20
69:17	20
69:19–29	20
69:30–36	20
69:25	20
69:26	20

Psalms (*continued*)

89	32
89:20–38	107
109:1	44, 45, 46
109:8	20
118:22	59
131:11	44
132:11	44

Isaiah

2:1–4	69
6	131
6:9	27
11:11–12	68
11:12–13	73
28:25–28	27
32:15	36, 41
35:8–9	54
40:3	67
40:5	67
41:9	78
43:5–6	68
43:24–25	49
44:3	36, 41
45:22	78
49:5–6	37, 56
49:6	37
49:12	68
53	77
53:7–8	76
55:3	109
56: 3–7	76
58:6–7	49
66:1	65
66:18–20	68

Jeremiah

5:28–29	
7:5–7	
31:17–10	73

Ezekiel

18:31	49
36:27	36
36:27–28	41
37	37
37:14	36, 41
37:15–28	73

Joel

2:1–13	27
2:12–13	49
2:17–21	27
2:28–29	36
2:28–32	42, 49

Amos

9:11–12	83

Micah

6:7–8	49

Zechariah

2:6	68
8:13	73
8:20–23	69
10:6–12	73

✦

NEW TESTAMENT

Mark

14:56–57	61
14:58	61
14:62	61
14:64	61
15:36	62

Scripture Index

Luke

1–2	31, 34
1:1	3, 14, 25
1:1–4	1, 8
1:3–4	9
1:4–5	43
1:5–25	32
1:6	35
1:16–17	48
1:20	20
1:21	20
1:31–35	43
1:32–33	32, 98
1:34–38	32
1:41–45	34
1:54–55	33, 39
1:67–79	34
1:68–69	84
1:72–73	33
1:76	48
2:4	32
2:10	67
2:11	33
2:25	33
2:25–28	39
2:30	131
2:30–36	35
2:31–32	33
2:32	67
2:34	33
2:38	34, 37
3:4–6	48
3:6	67
3:7	128
3:10–14	48
3:16	11, 12, 40
4:13	19
4:26	59
4:43	35
5:17–26	93
5:27–32	50, 80
5:35	24
6:12–16	4
6:14–16	39
6:20	35
7:36–50	50, 80
8:10	35
8:12	99
9:2	35
9:11	35
9:11–17	50
9:16	126
9:21–22	27
9:22	24, 25
9:27	35
9:31	25, 37
9:44	24
9:44–45	27
9:51	37
9:51–56	113
9:53	37
10:10–11	92
10:18–19	128
10:19	128
11:11–12	128
13	77
13:33	24
13:33–35	37
15:1–2	50
17:25	24
18:31–34	27
18:31	25
18:32	24
18:33	25
18:34	37
19:1–10	50, 77
19:11	37
19:28–40	98
19:38–40	34
19:41–44	34, 63
20:2	57
20:2–3	25

Luke (*continued*)

20:17	24
20:18	59
20:19	59
20:30–32	11
20:45–47	19
22:1–2	34
22:2–3	19, 25, 39
22:6	19
22:14–38	103
22:17	126
22:19	126
22:29	40
22:29–30	50
22:30	39, 40, 52
22:31	25
22:31–32	27
22:37	24
22:42	25
22:48	25
22:53	25
22:66–71	34
23:34	62
23:46	62
23:25	25
23:51	25
24:6	25
24:8–12	26
24:19	63
24:24–27	26
24:26	25
24:26–27	28
24:28–35	4, 26
24:30–35	50
24:31	89
24:36–53	12, 26
24:44	25, 28
24:44–49	26
24:47	37, 78, 80
24:47–49	67
24:49	4, 12, 40, 43
24:50–53	12, 43

John

4:9	72
4:19–26	72
8:48	72
20:30–31	9
21:18	124

Acts

1:1	1,3,8, 12
1:1–2	11, 39
1:1–8	26
1:1–11	11, 12, 34, 55
1:2	12
1:3	12, 99
1:4	12
1:4–5	12, 40
1:5	12
1:6	12, 34, 36, 55
1:6–8	40
1:6–11	36, 46
1:7–8	36
1:8	4, 5,12, 38, 40, 68, 69, 72, 78, 86, 138
1:9–11	43, 65
1:10–11	46
1:15–26	7, 27, 39, 52
1:16	27
1:17	39
1:18	4, 19, 50
1:20	27, 29
1:23	38

1:25	19	2:38	49
1:26	39	2:39	78
2:1–4	11, 41	2:40	49
2:1–13	5, 38	2:41	47,48, 49,
2:2	65		59, 70
2:2–3	41	2:41–47	49
2:3	68	2:42	49, 126
2:4	68	2:42–47	5, 50, 54,
2:5	65		70, 103,
2:9–11	68		124, 139
2:11	68	2:43	42, 49, 60
2:14–41	7	2:44	49
2:17	29,42, 78	2:44–45	48
2:17–21	42, 119	2:46	126
2:18	42	2:46–47	49
2:19	42, 60	2:47	59, 70
2:21	42	3:1–10	17, 47, 54,
2:22	40, 63		77
2:22–36	28, 43, 45,	3:1–26	119
	101, 108	3:6	47
2:23	25, 59	3:10	93
2:24	17, 26, 44	3:11–26	101
2:25	45	3:13	15, 16, 17,
2:24–35	26		47
2:29	44	3:13–14	63
2:29–33	109	3:14–15	53
2:30	44	3:15	17, 26, 38,
2:30–31	84		53
2:30–33	119	3:16	137
2:30–36	99	3:17	53
2:31–33	44	3:18	25, 53, 55
2:32	26, 38	3:19	53, 54
2:33	17, 45, 46,	3:19–20	36
	65	3:20	47, 53, 54,
2:33–35	17, 26		55
2:33–36	54	3:20–21	36
2:34	45	3:21	36, 54, 55
2:35	45	3:22	63
2:36	17, 46, 48	3:22–23	16, 55, 59
2:37–38	137	3:24	53, 55
2:37–47	48	3:25	78

Acts (continued)	
3:26	16
3:35	15
4:1–22	139
4:2	57
4:2–4	47
4:4	59, 70
4:7	57, 58
4:8	60
4:8–12	17, 57
4:8–31	69
4:9–10	47
4:10	26, 59
4:10–12	119
4:11	58
4:12	58
4:13	4, 58, 60
4:14	58, 60
4:16	42, 58
4:19	58
4:22	42
4:23–31	138
4:25	15, 16
4:25–28	26
4:27	17
4:28	26
4:29	60
4:29–31	58
4:30	17, 42
4:31	21, 60
4:32–35	5, 70, 103, 124, 139
4:33	60
5:1–11	4, 19, 139
5:12	4, 42
5:12–15	60
5:12–16	5
5:13	58
5:14	48, 70
5:15–16	58
5:17	58
5:19–20	5, 6, 21
5:20	59
5:27–32	101
5:28	58
5:29	58, 5
5:29–30	59
5:30	15, 17, 26, 59
5:30–31	119
5:31	17, 58, 63
5:31–32	138
5:32	38, 138
5:39	5
5:40	20
6:1	48
6:1–6	139
6:2	70
6:3	60, 70
6:5	60, 70
6:7	4, 48, 61, 138
6:8	4, 42, 60, 70
6:8–15	61
6:10	60, 70
6:11	61
6:11–15	15
6:12	61
6:13	61
6:14	61
6:18–15	4
7:2	71
7:9	71
7:11–52	15
7:17–37	16
7:17–43	62
7:22	63
7:22–23	71
7:23–26	63
7:25	42
7:27	63

7:30–33	71	8:26	74
7:31	63	8:26–40	77, 88, 139
7:32	15		
7:35	63	8:27	76
7:37	63	8:30–35	74
7:40–41	64	8:34	75
7:42	64	8:36	75, 76
7:42–43	64	8:36–38	49, 137
7:44–45	71	8:38	74, 75
7:46	15	8:38–39	76
7:48	64	8:39	74, 75
7:48–50	71, 120	9:1	12
7:49	76	9:1–19	29, 28
7:51–52	64	9:2	21
7:54	61	9:3	86
7:54–60	45, 61	9:3–12	42
7:55	65, 70	9:5	86
7:55–56	42, 71	9:10	86
7:55–60	65	9:11	86
7:59	62	9:13	86
7:60	62	9:15	22, 78, 86, 106
8:1	72		
8:1–3	74	9:15–16	87, 93
8:1–4	7, 21	9:17	86
8:4	72	9:17–19	49
8:4–17	139	9:20–22	22, 87
8:4–25	6, 74, 87	9:31	74
8:5	72, 73	9:35	55
8:6	4, 42	10	11
8:6–7	73	10:1–8	29
8:9–11	73	10:1–48	5, 86
8:12	35, 73, 99	10:1—11:18	6, 38, 78, 88
8:13	42, 73		
8:14	72, 74	10:3–6	79
8:14–24	18, 128	10:9	79
8:14–17	42, 73	10:15	79
8:15	72	10:9–16	29
8:18–24	97	10:17–19	42, 79
8:18–25	4, 19	10:20	79
8:24	75	10:22	79
8:25	72, 74		

Scripture Index

Acts (*continued*)

10:23	79
10:25–26	129
10:28	80
10:34	80, 139
10:36	17, 63, 81, 139
10:36–43	40
10:40	26
10:43	80
10:44–45	80
10:44–46	80
10:44–48	42
10:46	80
10:47	80
10:47–48	80
11:1–18	5, 81, 86
11:15–17	80
11:17	81
11:18	81
11:19	81
11:20	81
11:21	82
11:23	82
12:1–17	6
12:13–52	82
12:20–23	5, 18
12:22	94
12:24	4, 48, 138
13:1–3	87
13:1—14:20	102
13:1—14:28	87, 106
13:2	22, 88
13:4	102
13:4–12	18, 82, 97, 100, 128
13:4—14:28	22
13:13	102
13:13–41	106
13:14	107
13:15	16, 107

13:16	107
13:16–41	4
13:17	15, 84, 107
13:17–36	15, 24
13:18	107
13:19	107
13:20	107
13:21–22	107
13:23	44, 107, 108
13:26	107
13:30	26, 108
13:31	38
13:32	109
13:32–33	108
13:32–37	84, 99, 108
13:32–39	119
13:33	26, 109
13:34	26
13:34–41	16
13:37	26
13:38	107
13:38–41	109
13:42–52	110
13:43	110
13:44–45	110
13:44–52	131
13:46	47
13:46–47	111, 113
13:46–52	110
13:47	5, 37, 111
14:1	111
14:1–7	82
14:2	111
14:5–7	111
14:8–10	17, 93
14:8–18	91
14:8–19	129
14:8–20	82, 97

14:19	111	16:11—18:23	111
14:21–28	82	16:13	89
14:27	105	16:13–14	89
14:11	18	16:14	90
14:13	18	16:15	89, 90,
14:15	18, 95		137
14:16	15	16:16	90
14:17	95	16:16–18	19, 97,
14:18–19	95		100, 128
14:22	35, 102	16:18	98
14:23	102	16:19–34	90
15:1	82	16:20	90, 98
15:5	82	16:21	90, 98
15:6–11	5, 137	16:25	90
15:7	83	16:25–29	91
15:7–10	86	16:25–34	5, 6, 112
15:8	83	16:26	91
15:9	83, 88, 89	16:29	91
15:9–10	82	16:30	91
15:10	15	16:31	91
15:10–11	83	16:32	91
15:11	42, 80	16:33	91
15:12	83	16:34	91
15:13–21	83	16:40	90, 112
15:14	83, 88	17:2	112
15:14–18	80	17:2–3	92, 98
15:15	83	17:4	91, 112
15:16–18	83	17:5	91, 92
15:19–20	84	17:5–7	112
15:36—18:22	87	17:5–8	98
16:1–5	115	17:6	92
16:6	88	17:6–7	112
16:6–7	22	17:7	91, 92, 98
16:6–10	38, 88	17:12	112
16:7	88	17:12–15	112
16:8	88	17:16	100
16:9	22	17:16–34	4, 97, 100
16:9–10	42, 88	17:17	100
16:10–17	2	17:18	100, 101
16:11–13	102	17:22–31	5, 18
16:11–15	112	17:23	101

Acts (*continued*)

17:24	97, 101
17:24–25	101, 120
17:26	101
17:28–29	101
17:29	97, 101
17:30	101, 137
17:31	17, 26??
17:30–31	15
17:32–34	101
18:1–11	92
18:3	92
18:4	92
18:5–6	113, 131
18:5–8	112
18:6	5, 47, 92, 112
18:7	93
18:8	93, 112
18:9	93
18:10	93
18:12–13	8
18:14–15	118
18:24—19:41	87
19:5	96
19:8	35, 96, 99
19:10	96
19:11–12	96
19:11–20	128
19:13	96
19:17	96
19:18–20	100
19:20	4, 5, 96, 138
19:21	113
19:21–41	98
19:23–40	96
19:25	99
19:26–27	96
19:27	97
19:28	97

19:32	97
20:1–3	102
20:1–16	102
20:5–15	2
20:7	103
20:7–12	103
20:11	103
20:17–35	122
20:18–21	103
20:18–35	10, 102
20:19	104, 105
20:20	104
20:21	104
20:22–23	103, 104
20:23	113
20:23–25	131
20:24	104, 105
20:25	35, 103, 104
20:27	104
20:28	105
20:28–30	103
20:29–30	105
20:31	103, 105
20:32	105
20:33	104
20:34	104
20:35	104
21:1–15	102
21:1–18	2
21:4	103
21:5	103
21:7–8	103
21:7–17	127
21:9	103
21:10	103
21:10–12	113
21:11–14	103
21:13	131
21:13–14	113
21:17	114

21:17–26	120	26:30–32	121
21:19–21	114	27:1–28:10	121, 123,
21:20	48		130
21:20–22	115	27:1—28:16	2,6
21:24	114, 115	27:2	123
21:25	114	27:3	127
21:27–29	115	27:6	123
21:28	115, 120	27:8	123
21:29	115	27:9	123
21:30–36	115	27:10	124
21:31	115	27:10–11	124
21:32–33	117	27:14	123
21:36	115	27:18–19	123
22:1–3	117	27:20	124, 125
22:1–21	117	27:21	124
22:2	117	27:21–26	29, 124
22:6–10	86	27:22	124
22:6–11	119	27:24	123, 124,
22:7	119		125
22:14	15, 119	27:24–26	131
22:15	138	27:25	124
22:17–18	119	27:25–26	125
22:21	87	27:26	124
23:1–8	117	27:31	125
23:11	119, 131	27:33	125
23:29	118	27:33–34	124
24:10–21	117	27:33–37	125
24:14	15	27:33–38	126
24:14–15	117, 118	27:33	126
25:25–27	118	27:34	124, 125,
26:1–23	117		126
26:6	15	27:35	126
26:6–8	118	27:36	126
26:6–9	39	27:37	126
26:12–18	119	27:38	126
26:17–18	87	27:41	123
26:18	120	27:43	125
26:19–23	118	27:44	125
26:22–23	118	28:1	124, 125
26:27	117	28:1–2	100, 127
26:27–29	120	28:1–10	129

Acts (continued)

28:2	127
28:3–6	100, 128, 129
28:4	128
28:5	128
28:7	129
28:7–10	129
28:8	129
28:9	129
28:9–10	100
28:10	129
28:11–31	121
28:12–15	127
28:16–31	5, 121, 130
28:17–20	130
28:17	130
28:19	130
28:20	120, 130
28:21–22	130
28:23	130
28:24	130
28:25	131
28:25–27	131
28:28	42, 47, 122
28:23	35
28:25	15
28:28	5, 132
28:30–31	99, 132
31	35

Romans

15	2

1 Corinthians

16:1–4	2

2 Corinthians

8–9	2

Colossians

4:14	2

2 Timothy

4:10–11	2

Hebrews

1:5	44

Made in the USA
Columbia, SC
20 January 2022